HOW TO TOUR CHINA

Newest Comprehensive
Guidebook of China

CYPRESS BOOK COMPANY, INC.
Paramus NJ 07652, USA

and

XINHUA PUBLISHING HOUSE
Beijing, China

HOW TO TOUR CHINA
Newest Comprehensive Guidebook of China
First Edition 1986
Published by
XINHUA PUBLISHING HOUSE
57 Xuanwumen St. W., Beijing, China
and
CYPRESS BOOK COMPANY, INC.
Paramus Place, Suite 225, 205 Robin Rd., Paramus, NJ 07652,
USA
Distributed by
CHINA INTERNATIONAL BOOK TRADING CORPORATION
(GUOJI SHUDIAN)
P.O.Box 399, Beijing, China
Printed by
L. REX OFFSET PRINTING CO., LTD.
Man Hing Industrial Godown Bldg., 14th Floor,
No. 4 Yip Fat ST., Wong Chuk Hang, Hong Kong
ISBN 0-934643-00-8

CONTENTS

FOREWORD

You may have already searched through dozens of China guidebooks in your local bookstore. But this one, "How to Tour China", may be just what you are looking for — up-to-date, information-packed, beautifully ill-ustrated and handy to carry around.

The journalists of the Beijing-based "China Features" organization, all Chinese residents and experienced writers on such subjects as travel, history, art and sport, have put their heads together and come up with this comprehensive tourist 'how-to" book, one of the many books they have compiled about China.

They have racked their brains, and tried to answer all the questions a visitor to China could possibly ask.

Do you want to know whether China has any Yellowstone-type national parks? Where Bruce Lee's superb kung-fu originated from? How long the Great Wall is? What the open cities and Special Economic Zones are? What the life of a Mongolian nomad is like? Where to mingle with the ethnic groups in remote parts of southwest China? Where to get a real Peking Duck dinner? How to convert your extra local currency to your original currency? How much to pay for a taxi? How to ask for help? How to arrange your itinerary? When to see the spectacular Qiantang tidal bore?

It's all here in "How to Tour China", which covers almost all the major tourist cities, localities and beauty spots in China, and contains nearly all the relevant information you may need on your tour.

All the cities and tourist attractions are grouped according to their geographic locations, and then arranged in alphabetical order.

This book takes care of you from the point of planning your trip to the time when you want to leave China. And after you return home, it may help bring back many of the pleasant memories of your tour.

The Great Wall

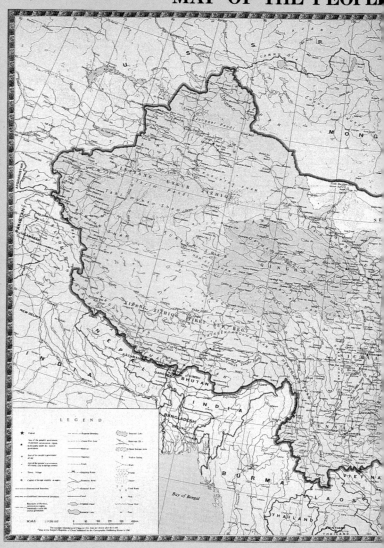

EPUBLIC OF CHINA

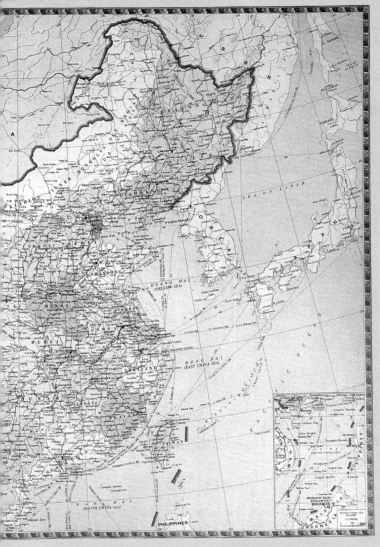

Former Imperial Palace

INTRODUCTION

China, once known as the Central Kingdom, still reigns as a land of beauty and fascination, which tempts adventurous travellers from all over the world. It is a massive country, covering 6,000,000 square miles — bigger than the United States, almost as large as the whole of Europe, and spanning 60 longitudinal degrees.

China has a most varied topography, with a terrain high in the west and low in the east. It has the world's highest peak — Mount Qomolangma on the China-Nepal border — and the world's lowest basin — at Turpan, in the Xinjiang Uygur Autonomous Region, which is 505 ft. below sea level. It has highlands in Tibet which are referred to as "the roof of the world". While there are vast deserts in the north-west, there is a long fertile coast in the east and south, washed by the Pacific Ocean, and irrigated by mighty rivers, such as the Yangtze, Yellow and Pearl.

As the greater part of the country lies in the temperate zone, seasonal differences are distinct, and the climate as a whole is mild, although it varies from desert to tropical. The most striking feature is the monsoon winds — the wet monsoons blowing landward from the Pacific and Indian oceans in the warm seasons, and the dry prevailing winds sweeping towards the sea in the winter. In general, it is temperate and humid in the southeast and central south, and rather dry in the north and northeast.

The growth of one of the world's richest cultures and most advanced civilizations can be traced over four turbulent millennia of written Chinese history.

The country is roughly divided into seven major geographic divisions: central, east, north, northeast, northwest, south and southwest China. There are 22 provinces (including Taiwan), five autonomous regions and three municipalities — Beijing, Shanghai and Tianjin.

Apart from the Han, the majority nationality, there are 55 ethnic groups, and the population, according to the 1982 national census, is 1,031 million. It is reckoned that by the end of this century, one person in every four on this planet will be Chinese.

TOURIST INFORMATION

PLANNING TO GO

The formalities to go through before setting off on your trip are quite simple. Besides buying your travel ticket, you must apply to a Chinese embassy or consulate for a visa to be stamped on your passport. Usually, you need an invitation to visit China, although there is no reason why you shouldn't apply for a visa before receiving the invitation.

INVITATIONS: You can get an invitation from nearly all major government bodies, organizations, institutions, or enterprises. Choosing the one you want to be your host depends on your interests and what you want to do in China.

As a tourist, however, the simplest and most reliable way of getting an invitation is to go to China National Tourism Administration, which has tourist offices in many major cities throughout the world, including New York, London, Paris, Tokyo and Frankfurt. You can always rely on the administration for help and advice.

VISAS:With the invitation at hand, or even before you have received it, you can apply for a visa for tourist or business purposes to the Embassy of the People's Republic of China in your country of residence. If you are out of your country, then you may apply to a Chinese embassy or consulate abroad. A list of some of the embassy and consulate addresses is given below.

As of January 1, 1985, foreign tourists can directly apply for a visa in the following nine ports: Beijing, Tianjin, Shanghai, Hangzhou, Fuzhou, Xiamen (Amoy), Guilin, Kunming and Xi'an.

Two copies of the application form should be completed and submitted with two passport-size photographs along with a visa processing fee. Normally, you are not required to submit your passport until advised to do so by the embassy. When filling in the application form, you will be required to state which places you wish to visit. When in doubt, add towns to the list rather than omit them, for once a visa is granted and you are in China, it is difficult to add new places but easy to delete them.

Major Chinese Embassies and Consulates Around the World

Country	Address
Australia	14 Federal Highway, Watson, Canberra, A.C.T. 2602 Tel. 412448
Austria	1030 Wien Vienna, Metternichgasse 4 Tel. 753149 Telex: 135794 CHINB A
Belgium	19 Boulevard General Jacques, 1050 Brussels Tel. 6482886, 6496773 Telex: 23328 AMCHIN B
Canada	415 St. Andrew St., Ottawa, Ontario, Canada KIN5H3 Tel. 2342706 Telex: 0533770

Consulate-General of the
People's Republic of China,
Town Inn Hotel,
620 Church Street,
Toronto, M4Y 2G2
Tel: (416) 9647575, 9647260

Consulate-General of the
People's Republic of China,
3380 Granville St.,
Vancouver, B. C. V6H 3K3
Tel. (604) 7363910

Denmark	Oregards Alle 25, 2900 Hellerup, Copenhagen Tel. (01) 625806 Telex: CHINEM 27019, Copenhagen
France	11 Avenue George V, Paris, 8 EME, France Tel. 7367790 Telex: 270114
Federal Republic of Germany	Kurfuerstenallee 12, 5300 Bonn-BAD Godesberg Tel. 361095, 96, 97 Telex: 885655
Italy	56 Via Bruxelles, 00198 Roma Tel. 8448186

Japan	(4-33, Moto-Azabu 3-chome, Minato-Ku, Tokyo) Tel. 403-7955, 403-3383
Mexico	Av. Rio Magdalena 172, Colonia: Villa Alvaro Obregon, Mexico 20, D.F., Mexico Tel. 5482821
Netherlands	Adriaan Goekooplaan 7, The Hague Tel. 547516
New Zealand	2-6 Glenmore Street, Wellington Tel. 721383
Norway	Tuengen Alle 2B, Vinderen, Oslo 3 Tel. 110053
Spain	C/Arturo, Soria No. 111-113, Madrid-33 Tel. (91) 4152031 Telex: 22808 EMCHI E MADRID
Switzerland	Kalcheggweg 10, 3006 Berne Tel. 031/447333
Sweden	Bragevägen No. 4, 114 26 Stockholm Tel. 217539 Telex: 19608 Hoating S

United Kingdom	31 Portland Place, London WIN3AG Tel. 6365637 Telex: 23851
United States	2300 Connecticut Avenue N.W. Washington, D.C. 20008 Tel. 3282515 Telex: 440038 PRC U1

United
Kingdom

31 Portland Place,
London WIN3AG
Tel. 6365637
Telex: 23851

United States

2300 Connecticut Avenue N.W.
Washington, D.C. 20008
Tel. 3282515
Telex: 440038 PRC U1

Consulate-General of the
People's Republic of China,
3417 Montrose Blvd.,
Houston, Texas 77006
Tel. (713) 5240780, 5240778

Consulate-General of the
People's Republic of China,
520, 12th Avenue,
New York, N.Y. 10036
Tel. 212-279-1127

Consulate-General of the
People's Republic of China,
1450 Laguna St.
San Francisco CA 94115
Tel. 415 563-4857

ARRIVING IN CHINA

Upon arriving at a port of entry, a foreign visitor must undergo passport, health, customs and currency formalities before entering China. The first control point you will encounter in China, like in many other countries, will check your passport to ensure that it is in order and that the visa entry is correct.

QUARANTINE: The second control point will check your health documents. Normally, no certificates or smallpox vaccination, or cholera or yellow fever inoculations are required, unless you travel from or via regions where such diseases have occurred recently.

But if you feel indisposed on the way to China, you should report, for your own good, to the Chinese frontier quarantine personnel at the airport, seaport or railway station of arrival.

CUSTOMS: At the third control point you and your baggage will be subject to customs formalities. You must fill in a baggage declaration form, on which all valuables should be listed, such as cameras, watches, jewellery, calculators, radios, tape recorders, typewriters, money and travellers' checks.

After inspecting your baggage against the declaration form, the customs officer will sign and stamp the form and return it to you. Keep this form safe, because your valuables will be rechecked when you leave China. Your valuables as listed should not be sold or given away, and any loss should be reported immediately to your host organization or CITS.

You are allowed to carry into China a limited quantity of duty-free goods and personal belongings, including two bottles of liquor and 400 cigarettes. Foreign liquor and cigarettes are now available at the "friendship stores" in many cities and shops in major hotels. These goods can be bought with foreign currency or foreign exchange certificate.

To make exit formalities smoother, please retain all invoices bearing the stamp "BOUGHT WITH FOREIGN CURRENCY" when you buy jewellery, jade, gold and silver ornaments, handicrafts, arts, paintings, calligraphy and similar items at the friendship stores or antique shops.

You must present to the customs at the time of exit a certificate for export of cultural relics issued by the Chinese authorities, without which you cannot take any such items out of China. Be careful to buy such cultural relics only with wax seals affixed by the Chinese Cultural Relics Administration.

You are not allowed to bring any weapons, drugs, poisons, pornographic materials, radio transmitter-receivers or Chinese currency into China. Travellers are allowed to bring into or out of China only their personal effects within the specified quantities stated in customs regulations.

A CUSTOMS GUIDE

I. BAGGAGE DECLARATION

1. Passengers on entering or leaving China should fill out a "Baggage Declaration" form and submit all their baggage for customs inspection.

2. Unaccompanied baggage should be specified in the "Baggage Declaration", and be imported or exported within six months from the date of entry or exit.

3. The passenger or his agent shall be present at the time of inspection.

4. Articles carried on behalf of others should be declared to the customs, who can levy any appropriate duties.

II. THINGS PROHIBITED FOR IMPORT

1. Arms, ammunition and explosives of any kind.
2. Radio transmitter-receivers and principal parts.
3. Renminbi (Chinese currency) banknotes.
4. Manuscripts, printed matter, films, photographs, phonograph records, moving pictures, recorded tapes and video tapes etc. that are detrimental to Chinese political, economic, cultural and moral interests.
5. Drugs.
6. Animals, plants and products thereof infected with or carrying diseases or insect pests.
7. Unsanitary foodstuffs and germ-carrying foodstuffs from infected areas.
8. Other articles whose importation is prohibited by state regulations.

III. THINGS PROHIBITED FOR EXPORT FROM CHINA

1. Arms, ammunition and explosives of any kind.
2. Radio transmitter-receivers and principal parts.
3. Renminbi and securities, etc. in Renminbi (Chinese currency).
4. Foreign currencies, bills and securities in foreign currencies (unless against a memo which records the foreign currency a foreign passenger brought into the country. Your extra Renminbi can be exchanged into the currency you want and can then be carried out).
5. Manuscripts, printed matter, films, photographs, phonographic records, moving pictures, recorded tapes and video tapes, etc. that contain state secrets or are otherwise prohibited for exportation.
6. Cultural relics and rare ancient books without a permit from the Chinese Cultural Relics Administration.

7. Rare animals, rare plants and their seeds without a special export licence.

8. Precious metals and stones and articles made thereof (with the exception of those within the quantity allowed to be taken out of China).

IV. DUTY-FREE ARTICLES FOR FOREIGN VISITORS

1. Reasonable quantities of clothing for personal use.
2. Foodstuffs not exceeding 93 pound per person.
3. Liquor — two bottles not exceeding 24 ounces a bottle in weight per adult.
4. Cigarettes not exceeding 400 per adult.
5. A wristwatch, cameras, radio sets, 8mm cine-cameras, 1/2-inch video recorders and other valuable articles for personal use, which must be taken out of China at the time of exit.
6. Cultural relics (with export permit issued by the Chinese Cultural Relics Administration and ancient works of handicraft art bought with foreign exchange certificates or travellers' checks or credit cards in foreign currency at Chinese friendship stores or cultural relics shops. But their total value should not exceed RMB 10,000 yuan (US$3,534).

CURRENCY, FOREIGN EXCHANGE, CREDIT CARDS AND TRAVELER'S CHECKS

The currency of the People's Republic of China is Renminbi (RMB), or "People's Currency", issued by the People's Bank of China.

The basic unit of this currency is the Yuan. A Yuan is divided into 10 *jiao*, and a jiao is further divided into 10 *fen*. The denominations are: one, two and five fen, in both notes and coins, one, two and five jiao in notes and one, two, five and 10 yuan in notes.

Upon arrival in China, you may convert your foreign currency, credit cards or travellers' checks into RMB in either Chinese banknotes or "foreign exchange certificates" (commonly known among the foreign community in China as wai hui at the Bank of China or at designated agencies at major airports and hotels, friendship stores and some antique shops which cater for foreigners. A piece of advice — change your foreign money into wai hui, which is acceptable everywhere, and do not change foreign currency with any individual, for black marketing in foreign exchange is strictly banned in China.

You may bring any amount of foreign currency into China. You are advised to keep the "exchange memo" given you by the bank or agency, because you will be required to present it when you convert the remainder of your Renminbi or wai hui back into your original currency before leaving China.

Here are the currencies which you can convert into wai hui or RMB: Australian dollar, Austrian schilling, Belgian franc, Canadian dollar, Danish krone, FRG mark, French franc, Japanese yen, Malaysian dollar, Dutch guilder, Norwegian krone, Singapore dollar, Swedish krona, Swiss franc, UK pound, US dollar and Hongkong dollar.

The following credit cards are acceptable in China: VISA, MASTER CHARGE, FEDERAL CARD, EAST AMERICARD-VISA, MILLION CARD, JCB CARD, AMERICAN EXPRESS and DINER. But they are accepted only at designated hotels, restaurants, cultural relics stores and friendship stores in Beijing, Shanghai, Tianjin, Guangzhou, Hangzhou, Nanjing, Wuhan and Kunming.

Travellers' checks and money orders from more than 30 foreign banks can be converted into RMB or foreign exchange certificates. For details, please contact the banks which have business relations with the Bank of China.

ADVICE FOR TOURISTS
—SOME DOS AND DON'TS

MEETING PEOPLE: Handshaking, once unthinkable for a Chinese woman, is now universal. It is correct to say: "ni hao?" ("how are you?'), although more familiar Chinese greetings include: "mang ma?" ("what's up") and "chi fan le ma?" ("have you eaten yet?").

Rather than try to remember the full, two-or-three syllable Chinese name, listen for the first one (equivalent to surname) and add "xian sheng" ("Mr."). Hence Liu Guoping becomes "Liu Xian Sheng". If you want to use the more intimate word, "tongzhi" ("comrade"), this is quite acceptable, although it may sometimes cause friendly laughter.

The Chinese often use occupational titles such as professor, doctor or engineer, and the terms "old" and "young" are employed to distinguish between people of the same surname. So 20-year-old Wang Ping is "Xiao Wang", while his father is "Lao Wang". (See SPEAKING THE LANGUAGE on page 163)

Don't be offended by the bluntness of Chinese smalltalk. It is quite common during a short chat with a new acquaintance to be asked how old you are, whether you are married and how many children you have.

IN THE STREET: Dress decently, eschewing bare torsoes plunging necklines or short shirts if you want to avoid even more attention than you will naturally attract as a foreigner. But T-shirts and blue jeans are quite common now, and you needn't worry about wearing them.

In small cities, you will be stared at, and in some outlying places, crowds may gather to look at the "waiguoren" ("foreigner"). It is only curiosity, and you will usually find people helpful to the point of embarrassment when it comes to queueing for buses, being served in shops or finding a seat in a restaurant.

GIFTS: As China opens its door wider and more foreigners are pouring in, the presentation of gifts is no longer taboo. Nevertheless, it is still a practice that requires good judgment and common sense. In general, it is quite acceptale at high official levels as a gesture of friendship between nations.

If you or your organization wish to distribute gifts of some value during your tour, keep in mind that local custom discourages the acceptance of gifts by individuals. But you can present them to an organization or group — to a school, factory, or the workers as a whole, to show your friendship with and interest in that organisation.

If you are to present books, you must take great care to study the contents before deciding that a particular book is a suitable gift. Books on history which contain any disparaging references to China will, if given, be returned. And books containing references or photographs contrary to the Chinese code of ethics and morals will only cause embarrassment.

The best guide in presenting gifts is: do not press them upon the recipients if there seems to be any reluctance on their part.

CHINESE TRAVEL SERVICES

There are three major state-owned travel services in China — the China International Travel Service (CITS), the China Travel Service (CTS) and the China Youth Travel Service (CYTS) — all under the National Tourism

Administration, the Chinese counterpart of a ministry of tourism.

CITS, as its name suggests, specializes in catering for foreign visitors. It has more than 100 branches or sub-branches in many Chinese cities, tourist centers, scenic resorts and border posts.

CITS's major functions are helping foreign tourists travelling in China, providing convention facilities, offering non-package tour services to foreign transit or individual travellers and foreigners residing in China.

Services include:
1. Guide-interpreter.
2. Airport and railway station transfer.
3. Travel arrangements in and outside China.
4. Baggage handling.
5. Processing entry, exit and transit visas and travel and residential permits.
6. Accommodation reservation and taxi hire.
7. Buying, booking and endorsing air, train and ship tickets.
8. Arrangement for customs declaration and clearance.

Preferential rates are offered to package tour groups of between two and 15 people, and still better rates can be obtained by larger groups between December and March 31. All details are obtainable from CITS.

The China Travel Service specializes in hosting overseas Chinese and foreign nationals of Chinese origin, while the China Youth Travel Service takes care of students and other young people visiting China.

TRAVEL REGULATIONS

Travelling in China can be an entirely different experience to touring Europe or the United States. But a basic knowledge of Chinese travel regulations can make the trip a lot smoother.

China has opened up more than 250 cities and counties to foreigners. With a valid visa, you may travel freely to 100 of these places without any separate travel permit. All the tourist centers described in this book, except Lhasa, fall into this category. (See the following list)

If you intend to visit other places, you must apply to the Chinese public security department for a travel permit. This, of course, can be arranged by CITS or the host organization.

If you intend to visit a Chinese place which at present is not open to foreigners, a special application must be made by the host organization with the province or region concerned. Such an application may take some time, so you are advised to let your host organization know your travel plan before you set out for China.

Taxis are available, but rent-a-car service is provided in only a few large cities. And foreigners are permitted to use their own cars for inter-city travel on the road between Beijing and Tianjin and in Fujian Province.

Regarding photography, the general principal is: "Wherever foreigners are permitted to go, they should be allowed to take pictures." But to avoid trouble, as elsewhere in the world, you are advised not to take pictures near military installations or from aircraft windows. Moving pictures and video tapes can be made, but only the 8mm cine camera and 1/2-inch video recorder can be carried by a foreign traveller.

In some museums, you are not allowed to aim your camera at rare cultural relics. Look out for a sign saying "No Photography" that will be prominently displayed.

Prostitution and black marketeering are strictly banned in China. So if you need to let a guest stay in your hote room, first contact the hotel reception desk, where you hav to fill out a form to state clearly your relationship with tha guest.

NIGHTLIFE AND ENTERTAINMENT

During your trip, you may fancy a break from sightseeing, shopping and making new friends. You may want to watch or take part in sporting activities, visit the theater or cinema, watch TV or simply enjoy some nightlife. The following details might give you a rough idea of what is available:

1. SPECTATOR SPORTS

In China's major cities, public sports competitions, international matches and demonstrations are held frequently. Ask your interpreter or anyone who knows English to translate the entertainment guide in the local press to find out what's on.

The most popular sports in China are soccer, basketball, table tennis, volleyball, badminton, ice hockey and gymnastics, plus the traditional Chinese sports of "Wushu" (martial arts) and "ying qi gong", in which special breathing techniques enable the athlets to perform amazing feats of strength and stamina.

As a rule, sporting events are held in the evening, usually starting around 19:00, and the admission fee is generally between one and two yuan (less than one U.S. dollar). Tickets are available from the box-offices on the day of the event or several days in advance for special attractions, such as the visits of foreign teams or the finals of national championships.

2. KEEP-FIT ACTIVITIES

If you are a keep-fit enthusiast, you will find plenty of company on your early-morning runs or limbering up exercises — jogging and wushu or taiji are popular every-where in China.

Also most major hotels have table-tennis and billiard rooms, and some places open to foreigners, such as Beijing's

26

International Club, have swimming pools and tennis courts.

The sports-minded tourists should bring tennis rackets in the summer and ice skates in the winter. Public skating is allowed on most big lakes in northern China. Even if you forget them, you can often borrow or rent them in China.

Public gyms, running tracks and sports pitches are open to foreigners, but mostly for competitions. For mere exercise, individual keep-fit fans should visit the international clubs or small gyms affiliated to some hotels.

3. THEATER AND CINEMA

Chinese theater in the mid 1980s is particularly lively, with the revival of many traditional operas and the emergence of new playwrights dealing with contemporary social issues. In addition, there are regular productions of foreign plays in Chinese and increasingly frequent visits by foreign companies, including ballet troupes and symphony orchestras.

Patience and the assistance of an experienced interpreter will help you to enjoy one of the most famous forms of Chinese theater — Peking Opera. It is a unique theatrical synthesis of song and dance, acting and acrobatics, which many foreigners and even some Chinese find difficult to understand.

Nevertheless, foreign eyes can feast on the sumptuous costumes and make-up and the acrobatic-oriented items, even though the plots may seem confusing.

Besides the world-famous Peking variety, there are many different provincial versions of the art throughout China. There are, for instance, "Yue Ju" in Zhejiang, "Yu Ju" in Henan and another form of "Yue Ju" in Guang-zhou.

Concerts, ballets and national song and dance performances are staged almost every day in the large cities.

Performances usually start at 19:00 or 19:30, and tickets for plays and shows are available from box-offices on the day or in advance from 09:00-11:30 and 13:00-17:00.

Cinema screenings are continuous (no entry during performance), with the last showing at around 23:00. There are no "adults only" films, and most foreign films shown in China are dubbed into Chinese. But sometimes in international clubs and other places of entertainment for foreigners, foreign films are shown in their original languages.

4. TELEVISION

TV broadcasts usually start at 19:00 with a 30-minute news program, including 10 minutes of world news, which is followed by various programs, including films, operas and live sports competitions.

Dancing

There are usually two or three channels in major cities. All are in Chinese, except for occasional background narrations in world news coverage.

However, in many big hotels, there are close-circuit programs of documentaries, usually about China's scenic wonders, national performing arts and sports, feature films and, occasionally, foreign films.

5. NIGHTLIFE

China's nightlife, in general, is hardly likely to set the pulses of most foreign visitors racing. But there are things to do apart from eating out and going to the cinema or theater. You might like to visit the Cosmos Club at the Great Wall Hotel, Charlie's Bar at the Jianguo Hotel, or the International Club in Beijing.

Dances are becoming a regular feature. Watch the notice boards in principal hotel lobbies for details. Drinks and disco music and/or a live band are always provided.

Some hotels offer billiards, 10-pin bowling, chess and card games, or even shooting and archery ranges. But there are no cabaret shows or casinos in China.

The parks also provide plenty of entertainment in summer — organized and spontaneous — including outdoor dancing contests.

100 TRAVEL-PERMIT-FREE CITIES AND AREAS

MUNICIPALITIES:
Beijing   Shanghai   Tianjin

OTHER CITIES AND AREAS (ARRANGED IN ALPHABETIC ORDER):

Anshan   Anshun   Anyang   Baotou   Beihai
Bengbu   Changchun   Changsha   Changzhou
Chengde   Chengdu   Chong'an county   Chongqing
Dalian   Dandong   Daqing   Emei   Fuoshan
Fushun   Fuzhou   Guangzhou   Guilin   Guiyang
Haikou   Hangzhou   Harbin   Hefei   Hengyang
Hohhot   Huangshan   Huizhou   Jiangling county
Jiangmen   Jilin   Jinan   Jingdezhen   Jining
(including Qufu county, Yanzhou county)   Jinzhou
Jiujiang (including Lushan Mountain)   Kaifeng
Kunming   Lanzhou   Leshan   Lianyungang
Liuzhou   Lunan Yi autonomous county
Luoyang   Nanchang   Nanjing   Nanning   Nantong
Ningbo   Qingdao   Qinhuangdao   Qiqihar
Quanzhou   Shantou   Shaoguan   Shaoxing   Shashi
Shenzhen   Shenyang   Shijiazhuang   Suzhou
Tai'an   Taiyuan   Tourist Destination of Jiuhua
Mountain   Tunxi   Urumqi   Weifang   Wenzhou
Wuhan   Wuhu   Wuxi   Wuzhou   Xi'an (including
Lintong county)   Xiamen   Xiangfan   Xiangtan
Xianyang   Yan'an   Yangzhou   Yanji   Yantai
Yichang   Yinchuan   Yueyang   Zhanjiang
Zhaoqing   Zhenjiang   Zhengzhou   Zhongshan
Zhuhai   Zuoxian

Tiananmen night scene

MAJOR TOURIST CENTERS

BEIJING (PEKING)

Beijing is the Chinese capital and a fascinating mixture of the old and new. It has been in existence as a settlement for more than 3,000 years, although the remains of "Peking Man" show that human life existed in this part of China half a million years ago. It has been a center of power under the Mongols, the Ming, the Manchu and now the People's Republic of China for a period spanning almost seven hundred years.

With an area of 6,870 sq. miles, it is today the political, cultural and administrative center of the People's Republic, which was founded in 1949, home of more than nine million citizens and seat of government.

31

One of the few inland capitals of the world not built on a major river, it owes its long pre-eminence to its strategic geographical position. Lying on the north-western fringe of the Great North China Plain, Beijing serves as a gateway to the Inner Mongolian steppes in the north, the Shanxi plateau in the west and, through the easternmost pass of the Great Wall at Shanhaiguan, to north-east China.

It first achieved prominence during the Warring States Period (475-221 B.C.). when it became the capital of the Kingdom of Yan and was called Ji (meaning "reeds", because of the marshy nature of the terrain).

The Mongolian emperor, Kublai Khan, renamed it Dadu (great capital) when he made it the base for his Yuan Dynasty (1271-1368 A.D.), but the first emperor of the succeeding Ming Dynasty moved his court to Nanjing (Nanking), where it remained until the third emperor returned the royal seat to Beijing.

Hence the name, Beijing, meaning "northern capital",

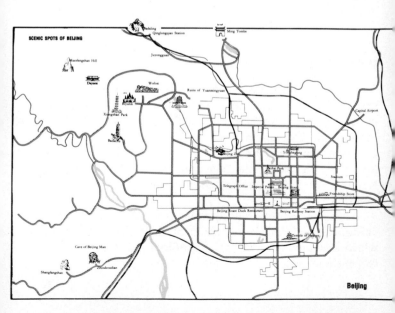

SCENIC SPOTS OF BEIJING

Beijing

Bicycle stream on the Changan Street

as opposed to Nanjing, which means "southern capital."

Since then, Beijing has always been the capital of the nation, except for a brief period during the civil war in the first half of this century, when Chiang Kai-shek's Kuomintang army again moved the government to Nanjing.

It was from the rostrum in Beijing's Tiananmen Square that, on October 1, 1949, the late Chairman Mao Zedong formally proclaimecd the founding of the People's Republic of China.

The historic Tiananmen rostrum is not only the symbolic heart of China, but also the key to Beijing. The whole city radiates out from it — or more exactly, from the grand royal compound of the Forbidden City — the old imperial palace — on the northern side of the square. The original city of Beijing was planned and for a time developed in such a way that the Forbidden City remained at the true center of the capital.

Hobby of old men-strolling with birds in the fresh morning air

Old meets new everywhere in Beijing—the ancient Forbidden City is overlooked by skyscrapers, the famous Great Wall pass north of the city proper is now surrounded by car parks, the centuries-old observatory stands next to a motor flyover, old court houses are dotted with glittering supermarkets, broad tar-paved avenues are flooded by millions of bicycles, ringing an echo of jingle bells, and damp underground tombs of the bygone emperors are illuminated by electric lighting.

Beijing is also the capital of Chinese cuisine, with many world-renowned restaurants where sumptuous banquets are served.

TIANANMEN SQUARE

Your tour of Beijing usually starts at Tiananmen Square in the heart of the city, a site of great political and historical significance.

The square, which can accommodate 500,000 people, is flanked by the Great Hall of the People to the west and the Museum of Chinese History and Museum of the Chinese Revolution to the east, with ancient Tiananmen Gate to the north. Chairman Mao Memorial Hall is in the south part of the square.

During festivities or political gatherings, the square is alive with people, red flags, lights and music.

During the Ming Dynasty (1368-1644) and Qing Dynasty (1644-1911), the square was only one-quarter of its present size, and was enclosed by a red wall. The only common people allowed to enter the enclosure were those being dragged in to be executed.

After the 1911 revolution that toppled the Qing Dynasty, the wall gates were demolished to let in the common people, and the square has since been the scene of many historic demonstrations.

The square was expanded to its present size after the founding of the People's Republic.

FORBIDDEN CITY

This quintessential symbol of traditional china lies in the heart of Beijing, just north of Tiananmen Square.

Built in the 15th century, the vast walled compound was the residence and seat of power of the emperors of the last two imperial dynasties — the Ming and the Qing. From the Dragon Throne there, they ruled the entire empire for five centuries with absolute authority. And inside the secluded Inner Palace, they lived in splendor, amid fabulous wealth amassed from the empire with their empresses and concubines.

The Imperial City was converted into a museum after the 1911 revolution, led by Dr. Sun Yat-sen, which toppled the Qing Dynasty. It now attracts 25,000 visitors a day.

The Forbidden City, which covers an area or about 180 acres, is a labyrinth of 9,000 rooms, zigzagging corridors and courtyards. Royal treasures and art works are on display in many rooms. The central feature of the city is the area containing the six Imperial Palaces set one behind the other along a north-south axis, where the emperors sat facing south and exercised their rule. On both sides are countless other buildings, and a miniature Imperial Garden is near the northern gate. From a raised spot in or near the city, you can have a breath-taking view of countless glazed-tile roofs glittering in the sun.

It could take weeks to explore the Forbidden City thoroughly, So be conternt to take in just what interests you the first day, and return for more if you are intrigued about something in particular.

TEMPLE OF HEAVEN

A park in southern Beijing, it is world-famous for its unparalleled architectural beauty. Here emperors used to worship Heaven, and pray for good harvests at the Temple of Prayer for Good Harvest, a conical structure built 564 years ago.

Temple of Heaven

THE SUMMER PALACE

The largest and best preserved of imperial Chinese gardens, it is only about half an hour by bus northwest of Beijing's city center. Known as the Summer Palace. or Yiheyuan, meaning Garden of Harmonious Unity, it served the court of China's last dynasty, the Qing.

For many years this scenic spot attracted pleasure-seeking feudal rulers, who adorned it with pavilions and gardens. Not until the reign of Emperor Qian Long (1736-95), the fourth Qing emperor, did the garden assume approximately its present size and shape. Qian Long named it Qingyiyuan, or Garden of Clear Ripples. Destroyed by fire in 1860 during the Second Opium War, it was rebuilt in 1888 by Empress Dowager Ci Xi who spent an enormous amount of money on it from funds appropriated for building a Chinese navy. Ci Xi named it Yiheyuan and made it her residence for the greater part of the year. In 1900 the palace gardens were again badly damaged when the combined forces of eight foreign powers pillaged Beijing. It was reconstructed in 1903 and opened as a public park in 1924, 13 years after the overthrow of the last imperial dynasty.

This palace garden occupies 716 acres, three quarters of which is water, mainly Kunming Lake at the foot of Longevity Hill (Wanshoushan), the focal point of the garden. One day is scarcely enough to see all the halls, towers, pavilions, corridors, walkways and bridges that grace the hill slopes, lake shore and islets. Though each has its own individual style, all blend harmoniously with the landscape.

MING TOMBS

Like Egypt's Pharaohs, the Chinese emperors of bygone dynasties were fond of building magnificent tombs for their "heavenly life". During the Ming Dynasty, 13 emperors built complexes of palatial buildings and

Tourists on the Sacred Way

underground vaults in the north-western suburbs of Beijing, where they were buried. These complexes were thus called the Ming Tombs.

They are located at 13 separate sites in a beautiful valley about 38 miles from central Beijing.

The main attractions are Ding Ling, tomb of the 13th Ming emperor, which was excavated in 1959 and is known as the "Underground Palace", and Chang Ling, tomb of the third Ming emperor and the biggest of the group. The sepulchre of Chang Ling has not yet been opened.

GREAT WALL

Though curiously unlisted as one of the seven wonders of the world, the Great Wall is undisputedly one of the World's engineering marvels.

It snakes along the Yanshan and Yinshan mountain chains that straddle northern China from east to west. Known in China as the "Ten Thousand Li Wall", it actually stretches 3,945 miles from Shanhaiguan pass at Bohai Bay on the Pacific Ocean in the east, to Jiayuguan, a stop on the "silk road", in the west.

It first took shape between the fifth and third centuries B.C. as a group of separate walls built by several northern warring states to ward off marauding nomads. When Qin Shi Huang conquered all the other six ducal states to become the first emperor of a united China, he ordered his men to link all these walls and extend them. It took 300,000 men 10 years to complete the construction. The connected wall was then further extended and improved by successive dynasties, the greatest renovation taking place in the Ming Dynasty, during which many sections of original earth structure was faced with bricks and stone.

For visitors staying in Beijing, the best place to see the Great Wall is a restored section at Badaling, about 37 miles from the city center.

Charming autumn scene of the Great Wall

The Haizhuqiao Bridge in Guangzhou

GUANGZHOU (CANTON)

Known as the "City of Goats", it is the capital of Guangdong province and the southern gateway to China. It is a pleasant city of tropical parks and tree-shaded streets, and also an important commercial center, with its port, Huangpu (Whampoa) being southern China's major foreign trading port, in close proximity to Hongkong and Macao.

The city proper, located on a bend of the Pearl River, is inhabited by 3,500,000 people, although greater Guangzhou, which includes six outlying counties, has a poulation of 5,500,000, and covers an area of 7,300 square miles.

The history of the city has long been associated with trade routes, which pass through the priovince and extend to distant lands, and which have made it a center for foreign commerce for more than 2,000 years. The first settlement is believed to have been established in the third century B. C. In the early Tang Dynasty (618-907 A. D.), an official "shipping company" was set up there, and since then, the city and the port have grown.

Guangzhou has played a prominent role in modern Chinese history. The Opium War of 1840, which marked the beginning of China's modern history, initially broke out there. Early in this century, Dr. Sun Yat-sen led several uprisings in Guangzhou to overthrow the feudal Qing Dynasty. The modern history of the city is now reflected in a number of famous historical monuments such as the Dr. Sun Yat-sen Memorial Hall, Mausoleum of the 72 Martyrs and Memorial Park to the Martyrs of the Guangzhou Uprising.

The city is located on the Tropic of Cancer, and has a warm and pleasant climate. The yearly average temperature is 22.1°C. July and August average 28.7°C, while January and February 13.2°C. Average annual rainfall is 1,800 mm

The mild climate and rich soil have made the Pearl River delta one of the most fertile parts of China. Subtropical fruit such as bananas, litchis and pineapples,

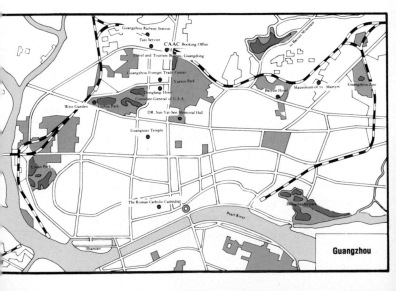

stock local markets, and the many flowers, which bloom the year round, have earned the city another name—the "City of Flowers". Around the city are half a dozen scenic spots featuring wooded slopes, lakes and ancient architectural buildings.

Guangzhou is connected with Hongkong by daily train, air, ship and hydrofoil services. The city's Baiyun Airport handles about 300 international and domestic flights a week. Railways link Guangzhou with all major Chinese cities, and the Huangpu Harbor, in the city's eastern suburbs, is one of the busiest ports in China.

GUANGZHOU FOREIGN TRADE CENTER

This building, formerly called the Exhibition Center, was opened in 1956 when the Chinese Export Commodities Fair (the Canton Trade Fair) was established. Covering an area of 131.560 sq. yd., it is large enough to display export items by the thousand, from art objects to heavy machinery, and gives the visitor an idea of the variety of goods produced in China. The center serves as a market where foreign buyers are introduced to the full range of Chinese goods available for export.

SHA MIAN ISLE

The isle is about half a mile long and 400 yd. wide. Two bridges (one a footbridge) span the canal that separates it from the city.

After the second Opium War, a foreign enclave was established there with permission of the Qing Dynasty. At that time, the isle was little more than a sandbar on the river. The English and the French furnished it with bulkheads and retaining walls of stone. In addition to private homes, a number of banks established branches and there were tennis courts and a sailing club for the residents.

Today, you will find the remains of walled gardens, malls lined with palms and a line of cannons aimed out over the river. The river bank, lined with banyan trees, is a lovely, cool place to walk. The large mansions are now government offices. This little isle now has a very tranquil, pleasant atmosphere.

THE ROMAN CATHOLIC CATHEDRAL

The cathedral was erected between 1860 and 1863 at which time it was consecrated. Designed in traditional gothic style, its pointed towers are 160 ft. high. The front elevation is 80 ft.; the overall length is 260 ft.; and the width 90 ft.

Mausoleum of 72 Martyrs

Located on Huang Hua Gang (Yellow Flower Hill), this mausoleum is a little over a mile outside Guangzhou. Covering approximately 192,000 sq. yd., it was built to commemorate the martyrs of the 1911 Revolution. Before Dr. Sun Yat-sen was triumphant in the battle against the Qing feudal rulers in October 1911, many uprisings had been waged but all had failed. In April 1911, 88 revolutionaries died in an unsuccessful revolt, and 72 of them are buried here.

The funds to erect this monument were collected from Chinese people in and outside China. Built in 1918, its design reflects a diverse number of influences. There are traditional Chinese lions, but also a small replica of the Statue of Liberty, an Egyptian obelisk, and a pavilion reminiscent of Versailles.

GUANGXIAOSI TEMPLE

This temple is one of the oldest in Guangzhou. Local legend has it that it existed before the city was established. Whatever the facts are, the temple is very old and has been damaged and repaired several times. An extensive restoration was carried out in 1832 and another is now under way.

The building bears the traces of a variety of different architectural influences, and the main hall is where these various styles seem to integrate most smoothly. When a school was being moved into the temple several years ago, three Buddhist statues were accidentally broken. These turned out to be hollow, and revealed inside little figurines of devout followers. Most of these, unfortunately, were lost, but those recovered are on display in a local museum.

WHITE CLOUD MOUNTAIN RESORT

This large mountain resort in the north-eastern suburbs of Guangzhou comprises more than 30 peaks in an area of 17 square miles. The main peak, although only 1,252 feet high, appears majestic, circled by clouds and mist for most of the year. Its densely-wooded slopes contain many historical sites. The peak is now accessible by car.

Making balls with strips of silk in Chaozhou Prefecture, Guangdong Province

Shanghai night scene

SHANGHAI

Shanghai contains the most striking blend of oriental and western cultures and of the past and present in China.

Tall old European-style buildings stand alongside low Chinese structures and ancient temples. Modern ocean-going vessels sail past junks. If you look carefully, you can still see the old names of banks and big foreign companies chipped into the stonework or written in faded paint on the facades of the western buildings that now house government offices. Old people still occasionally refer to the presentday People's Park as "The Race Course".

Shanghai is a flourishing commercial and industrial center. Its population of 11.8 million and its area of 2,355 sq. miles make it China's largest city, and one of the most populous cities in the world.

Although early records indicate that a settlement was

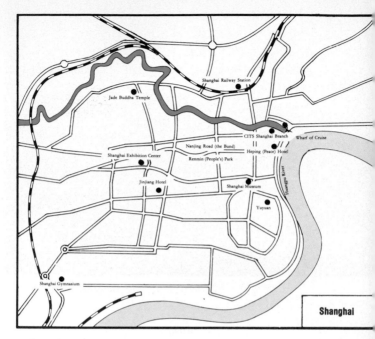

Shanghai

founded during the Song Dynasty (960-1280 A.D.), at a time when invaders from the north were drawing back to their own borders, it remained a small fishing village and did not become a town until the middle of the 13th century. Compared with other major cities in China it has had a relatively short history.

During the Ming Dynasty, many walls were erected to enclose the town and protect it from Japanese pirates. The town prospered from foreign trade in the Qing Dynasty. Prior to the outbreak of the Opium War, Shanghai had grown into a port with 500,000 inhabitants.

After the Opium War, Shanghai was forced by the European powers to open as a "treaty port". From that time on aggressors from many countries began to flock in and the city became known as a notorious "paradise for adventurers". Carving out their own spheres of influence, they settled there by seizing their respective "concessions", which was characteristic of this colonial period.

The Chinese response to this foreign dominance took several decades to become strong. On July 1, 1921, the First National Congress of the Chinese Communist Party was held in Shanghai, and the local residents as well as all of China began to fight back. During the war with Japan (1937-1945), Shanghai was occupied, and the Kuomintang regained it after the surrender of Japan. The city was taken by the people's army on May 28, 1949.

Since that time, Shanghai has changed from a consumer city of the past into a major industrial city.

Cultural activities include theater groups, film studios, a symphony orchestra, the ballet, opera companies, acrobatics and even a circus.

Because of the years of foreign influence, Shanghai, the first to open a disco for foreign visitors, is perhaps China's most cosmopolitan city. It also offers the tourist art and history museums tracing China's growth through the ages, and magnificent examples of Chinese architecture in its temples and buildings.

THE BUND

Your first wish on your tour of Shanghai will no doubt be to take a stroll along the Bund, or Zhongshan Road, and through the small parks along the river's edge. Here you will see citizens of Shanghai at rest, exercising, reading or practicing musical instruments.

You may want to lean on the sea wall and watch the bustle of the river traffic, one of the most interesting river scenes you will see anywhere in the world: a blending of wind and machine power on a very congested waterway. You will be fascinated by the navigating manoeuvres of diverse crafts.

Across the avenue from the river wall, the tall buildings that once housed the foreign mansions, clubs and banks are now occupied by state trading corporations, hotels, and one of the largest friendship stores in the country.

NANJING ROAD

Nanjing Road is Shanghai's busiest street. It starts at the Bund, south of the Peace Hotel, and runs west. It is the city's main shopping area with department stores, small shops, restaurants, theaters and cinemas. To the south of Nanjing Road is the Renmin (People's) Park. To the west you can see the Municipal Library, which was built in 1849.

Nanjing Road

Tourists on Jiuqu Bridge at Yu Yuan Emporium in Shanghai

YU YUAN

The Mandarin's Garden, as it is translated, was originally designed in the 16th century by the provincial governor, Pan Yunduan, in honor of his father, Pan En, who was himself a government minister. Construction took over 20 years. It is ingeniously laid out to imitate the style of imperial gardens in Beijing, and to create the feeling of spaciousness within a small area.

Yu Yuan is a garden within a garden. Divided into two parts, the outer garden contains pavilions, rock gardens and ponds, and leads to the inner garden, which is a smaller version of the outer one, consisting of many closely-packed pavilions. It suffered extensive damage over the years, but was restored in 1956.

Not only is it distinguished by its beautiful grounds, in southern Chinese style, but Yu Yuan has political significance as well. In the outer garden, you will find a small

49

museum, called the Beautiful Spring Hall, which was built to commemorate the Society of Little Swords. One of the loveliest spots in the Garden, it was used as the Society's headquarters during the 1853 Uprising.

XI JIAO PARK (Shanghai Zoo)

This zoo is situated in a western suburb of Shanghai near the airport and occupies an area of nearly 200 acres. The birds and animals on display here represent over 300 species and number more than 2,000. Among them are such rare Chinese birds and animals as the giant panda, golden monkey, red-crowned crane, northeastern tiger. Asian elephant, and Chinese alligator. There are also rare specimens from other parts of the world.

GARDEN OF THE PURPLE CLOUDS
OF AUTUMN

This park lies directly at the back of the Temple to the Town Gods, and contains an ornamental pond with landscaped hills surrounding it. Because of location, it is commonly referred to as the Inner Garden. It was originally laid out during the Ming Dynasty, and later acquired by a rich merchant. Finally, the town itself took over the park in 1726 as an additon to the Temple.

CHENGHUANGMIAO (Temple to the Town Gods)

The temple, or Chenghuangmiao, is only a short distance from Yu Yuan. Once every city and large town possessed a temple to the town gods, but few have survived.

HUANGPU RIVER CRUISE

The Shanghai Pujiang Cruise Service Station has boats of various sizes for sightseeing cruises on the Huangpu River down to its estuary into the Yangtze. Evening cruises are provided in summer. Bookings can be made through the Shanghai CITS office or at the station near Huangpu Park.

Distribution of China's tourism areas

TOURIST HIGHLIGHTS   1. CENTRAL CHINA

CHANGSHA

Changsha, located on the Xiangjiang River, is the capital of Hunan province. The city has a long history. A large town during the Spring and Autumn and Warring States Periods (770-221 B.C.), it was called Qingyang. In 221 B.C., after the first emperor of the Qin Dynasty unified China, the Changsha prefecture was set up. The city was opened to foreign traders in 1904. Europeans and Americans quickly moved into the area to establish businesses and warehouses. These merchant activities were boosted in 1918 when the town was linked by rail to Hankou and then Beijing, the development spurring an increase in production from the light industrial sector, particularly in food products, textiles, paper, lacquerware, jewellery and furniture. Changsha then became an important port for the export of agricultural products grown in the province, such as rice, tea, cotton, tobacco, hemp, and timber. Agriculture has always played an important part in its history. The land is very fertile, and even a drought cannot do much damage as water from the river can be diverted to irrigate the fields.

THREE HAN TOMBS OF MAWANGDUI

The Han Dynasty burial mounds of Mawangdui, meaning literally "King Horse's Hill", located in an eastern suburb of Changsha, date back about 2,100 years. They were excavated in early 1972. One contained the remains of an old woman. It is known as the Number One Tomb. The Number Two Tomb was occupied by her husband, who is believed to have died in 186 B.C. Since the tomb had been robbed, the corpse had rotted and many of the burial objects removed. Number Three appears to have contained their son. He died 18 years after his father, in 168 B.C. In the Number One Tomb, the corpse of the 50-year-old woman was in an excellent state of preservation. Her body had been wrapped in more than 20 layers of silk and linen. There was a silk painting draped over the inside of the coffin depicting scenes of life at that time and others from legend.

Archaeologists discovered more than 3,000 relics, including lacquerware, wooden figurines, bamboo books, pottery, a musical instrument not known today, bamboo baskets containing clothes and food, flutes and a bronze mirror. The body and a portion of the relics are now on display.

TAOHUAYUAN (Peach-Flower Spring)

A six-hour excursion west from Changsha will take you to Taohuayuan. It is so named because of its peach-tree-flanked spring. In ancient China, this was believed to have been a place of tranquility and happiness, and a heaven from the troubled world - a vision captured in the classical essay, "The Land of Peach flowers", by Tao Yuanming, a poet who lived 1,400 years ago. The present-day Taohuayuan bears a close resemblance to Tao's description. Located in a remote and tranquil area, it comprises, among other things, a clear stream, a beautiful grove and a cave.

ZHANGJIAJIE NATIONAL PARK

China's first Yellowstone-type national park, Zhangjiajie was set up in 1983. Located in western Hunan province, it covers 32,940 acres of virgin forest in a mountainous region. There are steep cliffs and clear springs, and wildlife is abundant.

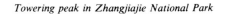

Towering peak in Zhangjiajie National Park

The Iron Pagoda in Kaifeng

KAIFENG

Situated on the southern bank of the Yellow River, Kaifeng is an important city in Henan province, covering an area of 219 square miles with a population of half a million.

With a recorded history close to 3,000 years, Kaifeng is known as one of the six major centers of ancient Chinese civilization. As early as the Yin-Shang period (1324-1066 B.C.), when Chinese society turned away from nomadic life to an agricultural existence, a city was built there. It then became the capital of the Kingdom of Wei in the Warring States Period (475-221 B.C.), the Liang, JIn, Han and Zhou dynasties of the Five Dynasties (907-960), the Northern Song Dynasty (960-1127) and the Jin Dynasty (1115-1234). The Northern Song, in particular, established its capital in Kaifeng for 168 years. The Eastern Capital, as Kaifeng was then called, was the political, economic and cultural center of the whole country, with well-developed handicrafts, bustling commerce and good communication facilities. An old saying went that "Kaifeng was unsurpassed anywhere in splendor

54

and prosperity".

Repeated Yellow River floods, however, caused damage to the ancient capital of Kaifeng, and many of its historical relics were destroyed. Among those that have survived are the "Iron" Pagoda, Pota Pagoda, Dragon Pavilion, Xiangguo Monastery, King Yu's Terrace and Yanqing Taoist Temple. These are all fine works of architecture. Their majestic beauty bears testimony to the wisdom and the high cultural and artistic level their creators attained.

The city today has well-developed commerce, transport, communications and educational facilities, and medical and public health services. The Yellow River that flooded its banks and wrought havoc for a thousand years has been harnessed. The Liuyuan Ferry at Kaifeng is now open to tourists as a scenic spot.

JEWISH COMMUNITY

Believe it or not there is a Jewish community in Kaifeng made up of several hundred Chinese Jews. The ancestors of these jews were said to have arrived in China from Persia and India during the Tang Dynasty.

For centuries, the Jews of Kaifeng uttered the prescribed daily and sabbath prayers, kept their religious holidays and observed strict diets.

SONG CITY

Kaifeng was a Song Dynasty capital for many years. Ask your guide to take you to the "Song City", a street flanked by small shops and taverns a thousand years ago.

The street is now under reconstruction on the old Imperial Street between the ancient imperial palace and another street called Sihoujie.

The palace has already been restored, and is open to the public. And another major part of the street, Xuandemen, will soon be completed.

Gate of Shaolin Temple

SHAOLIN TEMPLE

Located in the Songshan Mountains, a littel more than 50 miles south-west of Henan's provincial capital, Zhengzhou, Shaolin Temple is famous not only as one of China's important Buddhist shrines, but also as the ancient center of Chinese kung-fu.

Built in 495, the temple was originally designed to house Batuo, a celebrated Indian monk, who, after long years of spreading Buddhism, was later known as Fo Tuo, or Grand Monk. In 527, another famous Indian monk, Boddhidharma, settled in the temple, and, as legend has it, created a sort of primitive bare-hand combat routine called "xinyi boxing" after he had sat meditating in a cave for nine years.

That started the kung-fu tradition at the temple. At the beginning of the seventh century, a tiny army of 13 Shaolin monks were reputed to have saved future Tang Dynasty emperor Li Shimin, by defeating an entire division of the ruling Sui Dynasty's army and helping him break out of prison. When he took power, Li showered favors, land and wealth on the temple. Shaolin then thrived as a center of kung-fu, drawing kung-fu masters from around the country. At its heyday, it housed more than 2,000 soldier-monks.

Always a center of rebellion, Shaolin was badly damaged by fire three times, most seriously in 1928, when a blaze raged for more than 40 days, destroying nearly all the temple's classical literature and records.

The present buildings at Shaolin Temple are spread out over an area of about 10,000 acres. The most interesting relics are the murals in the Eastern Hall, which depict groups of boxing monks.

Forest of Pagoda in Shao Lin Temple

Peony of Luoyang is best of Heaven

LUOYANG

Luoyang, a city in Henan province, is situated on the north bank of the Luo River. The town is cut by two rivers which flow into the Luo: the Jian to the west and Chan to the east.

Henan is the heart of ancient China. As far back as the Neolithic Era (6-5,000 B.C.) the area was well populated. The capital of the bronze-age Shang Dynasty was located in the north, not far from luoyang, at present-day Anyang. Then in the llth century B.C., one of the Zhou kings made his temporary capital at Luoyi near Luoyang. Later, in 770 B.C., the eastern Zhou Dynasty rulers set up their capital at another site in the Luoyang area. Settlements in and around Luoyang were capitals for many periods until 937 , a period of more than 2,000 years.

Since 1949, the city has grown in importance as an industrial center. It now has machine-building works, chemical factories, textile plants, glass works and a large tractor factory.

LONG MEN CAVES

About eight miles south of Luoyang on the Yi River, at a spot where high cliffs on either side form a pass, is a caved area once known as the "Gate of Yi River", which later became known as Longmen, or the "Dragon Gate", after the Sui Dynasty emperor who was in those days worshipped as a dragon. Crafts men began work on Buddhist grottoes in 494 when an emperor of the Northern Wei moved the capital from what is now known as Datong (Shanxi province) to Luoyang. The artistry is therefore an extension of that evident in the Buddhist caves at Yungang just outside Datong. The work at Longmen proceeded through seven dynasties, and in more than 1,300 caves, there are 40 small pagodas, and almost 100,000 Buddha statues ranging in size from one inch to 57 feet. These caves and the stone sculptures they contain rank with the caves at Yungang and Dunhuang as the great remaining masterpieces of Buddhist culture in China.

Long Men Caves

NANCHANG

Nanchang is the capital of Jiangxi province, located on the Ganjiang river. Although it was settled as far back as the Han Dynasty (206 B. C.-220 A. D.), it remained for many centuries a storage and distribution center for the famous porcelain from nearby Jingdezhen. However, in 1927 it became famous throughout China when, on August 1, Zhou Enlai and Zhu De staged an uprising against the troops of Chiang Kai-Shek at Nanchang, before retreating to the nearby Jinggang Mountains to form one of the first armed forces to the Chinese Red Army. Today, the anniversary of the uprising is celebrated each year in China as the founding day of the Chinese People's Liberation Army.

There are few ancient historical sites of interest in Nanchang. You can join excursion tours there to the famous summer resort, Lushan Mountain, and China's porcelain capital Jingdezhen.

LUSHAN MOUNTAIN RESORT

Lushan is 95 miles north of Nanchang, at the center of

Lushan Mountain landscape

an area covering many scenic spots in the middle and lower reaches of the Yangtze River.

Lushan has been praised for centuries. Far back in the Han Dynasty (206 B. C.-220 A. D.), China's great historian, Sima Qian, wrote in his classic, "The Historical Records": "I mounted Lushan in the south and examined how Yu the Great had dredged the nine streams". It has inspired many poets and scholars of past dynasties to compose numerous works.

The scenery in the Lushan tourist area is lovely, and historical relics there are abundant. Up in the mountains are towering peaks, steep gorges, overhanging cliffs and cascading waterfalls. Due to the surrounding high mountains, thick forests, rivers and lakes, Lushan has long springs and cool summers, which make it a celebrated summer resort. At the foot of Lushan mountain lies the biggest freshwater lake in China—Poyang Lake, the recently-discovered karst cave Longgongdong, the Shizhongshan Hill and the ancient city of Jiujiang. All of them possess unique charms.

JINGDEZHEN

Jingdezhen, long hailed as the "capital of porcelain", is 75 miles north of Nanchang.

It has a long history, and was one of the Four Great Towns of ancient china. It covers an area of 2,021 square miles, and has a population of 611,030.

Porcelain was first made there during the Han dynasty (206 B. C.-220 A.D.). Since the Tang Dynasty, the white glazed china produced there had earned the name, "artificial jadeware". By the time of Emperor Jingde of the Northern Song Dynasty, when officials were assigned by the emperor to the town to supervise the manufacturing of porcelain for the royal families, Jingde china had won fame abroad. In the following centuries, it was sold to many countries across the world.

Jingdezhen, capital of porcelain

Since the founding of the People's Republic in 1949, a major pottery and china industry has developed.

Jingdezhen, with a mild and cool climate, is at the same time an interesting tourist resort. It nestles in mountains and is encircled by the Yangtze River. The visitor can see lovely lotus blossoming in the Lianhuatang Pond and enjoy the sweet scent of osmanthus from the Wufengge Pavilion. There is a famous ancient kiln at Hutian, and an ancient Ming street at the Sanlumiao. The newly-constructed exhibition ground for the display of ancient porcelain industry, called the Guzhen kiln, is of great interest. The Pottery and China Pavilion, the Pottery and China College, the Pottery and China Institute and more than a dozen major china manufacturing works are also well worth seeing.

WUHAN

This capital of Hubei province, lies at the confluence of the Yangtze and Han rivers, roughly midway between Beijing and Guangzhou.

The city is actually comprised of three towns—Wuchang, Hankou and Hanyang—that face each other across the rivers and are linked by two great bridges.

The area was first settled more than 3,000 years ago, and in the Han Dynasty about 2,000 years ago, Hanyang became a fairly busy port. In the first and third centuries A. D., walls were built to protect Hanyang and Wuchang. About 300 years ago, Hankou became one of the country's top four trading towns.

Since early this century, Wuhan has become well known as a center of revolutionary activity. The movement led by Dr. Sun Yat-Sen that resulted in the overthrow of the Qing Dynasty in 1911 began there. The town's workers were in the forefront of the national strike in 1923. The Central Peasant Movement Institute, where Mao Zedong taught Communist theory, was established there in 1926.

There are many memorial structures devoted to the revolutionaries, such as the Red Building, which housed the National Revolutionary Army Government in the 1911 movement, the Monument to the Martyrs of the February 7 Strike as well as the Central Peasant Movement Institute.

YANGTZE BRIDGE

The Yangtze Bridge at Wuhan was the first to be built across the mighty Yangtze River at this point. Including its approaches, it is 5,511 feet long, and carries a motorway and double-track railway.

Construction of the bridge started on September 1, 1955, and was completed on September 25, 1957, providing a throughway for traffic between north and south China.

Huanghelou (Yellow Crane Tower)

HUANGHELOU (Yellow Crane Tower)

Near the southern end of the bridge is Huanghelou, perhaps China's most badly-treated tower. It is said to have been built in 223 during the Three Kingdoms period. In the centuries that followed it was destroyed and then rebuilt several times. However, it inspired many ancient poets and artists, and local authorities rebuilt it in 1984.

GUI YUAN TEMPLE

This ancient Buddhist temple, an example of classic architecture commonly seen in southern China, has a history of more than 300 years. Inside is a huge hall containing 500 Luohans (small buddhas also known as arhats) in different postures, each with an individual facial expression. Some look experienced and astute, others jolly, angry, or complaisant—all fairly true to life.

East Lake

EAST LAKE

This is vast and so full of bays and gulfs that it has come to be called the "Lake of 99 Bays". The water is so clear that you can easily see the bottom. The scenery around the lake is lovely, with flowers and trees, pavilions and terraces.

WUDANGSHAN MOUNTAINS

A trip to Wudangshan mountains is a very worthwhile outing from Wuhan. Located in western Hubei, Wudangshan is an ancient sacred taoist shrine.

The first taoist temple there, the "Five Dragon Temple", was built 1,300 years ago in the Tang Dynasty. In the 15th century, the Ming court sent 300,000 soldiers and workers there to build 160 monasteries, temples, pavilions and other structures. It took them more than 10 years to complete the construction. It then became a major center of taoism. Although many of the old structures decayed in the following centuries, there are still many well-preserved temples.

The mountains are also linked with martial arts. It is said that Taiji boxing was invented there by a taoist priest.

65

Spring in West Lake

HANGZHOU

Hangzhou, the capital of Zhejiang province, lies close to the mouth of the Qiantang River at the western extremity of the huge estuary of the Gulf of Hangzhou.

Two thousand years ago there was nothing there but a sandbar built up by the silt carried downstream by the river. It collected between two fingers of land that jutted into the estuary. The inhabitants built a dike to reinforce the bar, and thereby created what is present-day Xi Hu, or West Lake, perhaps the most famous lake in China.

The settlement remained a small fishing village until late in the six century, when the extension of the Grand Canal southward from the Yangtze led to the development of a busy commercial center in the town. It prospered, especially during the tranquil early period of the Tang Dynasty, and its growth was assisted by the development of the lower Yangtze area into the nation's most important agricultural region.

Hangzhou underwent dramatic development when the Song Dynasty soldiers pushed south by the conquering Jin, established their capital there. In the short space of 100

2. EAST CHINA

years, the population increased to almost a million people and the town flourished as a major trading center. Even though parts of Hangzhou were destroyed during the late 13th-century invasion by the Mongols, the city, when visited by Marco Polo a short time afterwards, was still impressive. He said: "it is without doubt the finest and most splendid city in the world ... the streets and water courses alike are very wide ... there are said to be 12,000 bridges, mostly of stone ... vast are the numbers of those accustomed to dainty living, to the point of eating fish and meat at one meal."

As for West Lake, Marco Polo said: "On one side it skirts the city ... and ... commands a distant view of all its grandeur and loveliness, its temples, palaces, monasteries, and gardens with their towering trees, running down to the water's edge. On the lake itself is the endless procession of barges thronged with pleasure-seekers ... their minds and thoughts are intent upon nothing but bodily pleasures and the delights of society."

Today, the city remains renowned for its beauty, which some claim is unsurpassed in China; and although some of the historic buildings have been destroyed, the archaeological attractions that remain are still impressive. Many sections of the town have not changed for centuries, while the famous West Lake region retains its reputation as one of the best-known beauty spots in China, with landscaped gardens on its banks, tree-shaded walks, and in the nearby hills, temples, pagodas, and monasteries.

WEST LAKE

Hangzhou's fame rests mainly with the picturesque West Lake, so named because it is located on its western fringe. Covering about four square miles, West Lake is surrounded on three sides by rolling wooded hills. At the center are three isles—Lesser Yingzhou, Mid-lake Pavilion and Ruangong Isle. Solitary Hill stands by itself on the northern lake shore. It can be reached from the city by Bai Causeway, while Su Causeway bisects the lake from north to south. The blue, often rippling, water is dotted with elegant stone bridges and charming pavilions.

LINGYIN TEMPLE

It is believed that the temple was first established in 326 A. D. by a monk known as Hui Li. It was destroyed on a number of occasions, the last time during the Taiping Rebellion, and the latest rebuilding was in the early part of this century. The temple fell into disrepair, but in 1956 it was carefully restored.

The temple is set at the foot of the Northern Peak in a wooded area, a stream running before it. Some of the trees in front are believed to be more than 1,000 years old.

The foremost temple houses a laughing Buddha carved in camphorwood and covered in gold with a carved gilt figure standing behind as a guard. Both figures are set under a two-eaves wooden canopy decorated in red and gold. Ornate lamps hang on either side.

QIANTANG TIDAL BORE

If you are visiting in September during the autumn equinox, you may be able to see one of the most unusual sights in the world. A tidal bore gathers momentum in the Gulf of Hangzhou, surges into the mouth of the Qiantang River, and races up the river, at a height of up to 30 ft. and a speed of more than 15 m. p. h. In ancient times the governors of Hangzhou used to have arrows fired at these waves in an attempt to quell their destructive force. Nowadays more effective methods are used.

HUANGSHAN MOUNTAIN
(YELLOW MOUNTAIN)

Huangshan is located south of the Yangtze River in Anhui province. The mountain is magnificent with many peaks. Its natural landscape has remained largely untouched except for the construction of some roads and houses.

Huangshan is memorable for its clouds and changes in weather. Sometimes seas of clouds enshroud the peaks,

Scene known as "Meng Bi Sheng Hua" on Mount Huang

leaving only the tops peeping out like islands. Its pine trees grow in rock crevices in grotesque forms. The steep peaks are comprised of piles of strangely shaped rocks, split by deep secluded ravines. The static pines and rocks against the restless, moving clouds create changing scenes of great natural beauty.

Hot Springs: water from the springs is odorless and good to drink. It contains minerals beneficial in the treatment of gastric ailments, skin afflictions, and rheumatism. Hot Springs is one of the many attractions of Huangshan. Gushing forth from the foot of Purple Cloud Peak, the springs never run dry even during the most severe droughts, nor overflow their channels during excessive rains. All the year the temperature of the water remains at 104° F (40° C). Pools have been built for drinking, swimming, and medicinal baths.

Lianhua Feng *(Lotus Flower Peak)*: this towers above all the others, being the highest peak with an elevation of 6,138 ft. Famous pines such as the "Flying Dragon" and the "Twin Dragons" are found there. From the summit the neighboring peaks look dwarfed and in the distance the whole scene gradually merges into one shade of color.

Meng Bi Sheng Hua (Tip of a Magic Writing Brush): rising out of the profusion of trees and flowers, it is a pillar of stone tapering into a sharp point on which stands a twisted old pine. People metaphorically describe it as the "Tip of a Magic Writing Brush", that is, a brush painting all the lovely scenes of Huangshan.

Shixin Feng *(Beginning to Believe Peak)*: unlike some of the others, this peak is small and dainty but it has a charm of its own. It is noted for its gorgeous greenery and quaint rock shapes. The beauty of Huangshan is so captivating that one can't help feeling as if one has stepped into a Chinese landscape painting, exclaiming: "Now I believe it". Hence the name, "Beginning to Believe".

JINAN

Jinan, capital of Shandong province, is on the southern bank of the Yellow River, north of the famous Mount Tai. The Beijing-Shanghai and Qingdao-Jinan railways meet there.

The area was inhabited as far back as the Neolithic Period. Over 2,600 years ago, walls were built to enclose the town, which was then called Lu. The name was changed to Jinan 2,100 years ago because it was located to the south of the ancient Jishui River. In 1116, Jinan was established as a prefecture, and in 1368 it became the provincial capital. Jinan was incorporated as a city in 1929.

For centuries, the city has been renowned for its lakes and springs, including Daming Lake, and "The First Spring under Heaven", Baotu Springs.

The most exciting sights on your trip to Jinan, however, are probably the excursions to Qufu, the birthplace of the ancient philosopher, Confucius, and Mount Tai, the best of the country's "Five Sacred Mountains".

TAISHAN (Mount Tai)

Taishan, more than 345 miles in circumference, rises steeply and majestically in the middle of Shandong province about 45 miles from Jinan. Massive and awesome, it has featured in many historic events throughout the ages, and has been a rich source of inspiration for countless maxims, poetic allusions, and literary works. To many people this mountain is a symbol of grandeur and stability as shown, for example, in the popular Chinese saying, "Stable as Mount Tai".

Tiankuang *(Celestial Gift)* Hall: Tall and imposing, this main hall of the Dai Temple consists of nine rooms with double eaves, eight cornices and yellow glazed tile roofs. The

Cable cat completed in March, 1983.

frescoes (10ft. high and 170 ft. long) of life-like figures, covering the east, west, and north walls are rare, outstanding works of art.

Jinshiyu Valley: Half a mile to the northeast of Doumu Palace is a huge wall of rock (one 15th of a hectare) bearing an engraving of the Diamond Sutra. Each character is more than a foot high. The forceful calligraphy of this ancient inscription is regarded as the prototype of the bank (placard) style.

Nantianmen Gate: This is opposite the Beitianmen Gate (the Northern Celestial Gate) and can be reached by a steep, winding staircase. At the top is Mokong (Touching the Sky) tower with a stone tablet bearing an inscription by Du Renjie, a poet of the Yuan Dynasty.

QUFU

A 30-minute bus ride east from the Yanzhou railway station on the Beijing-Shanghai line (about 65 miles from Jinan) takes you to Qufu, the birthplace of Confucius. The first thing you will see is the spacious temple of Confucius, which dominates the town.

Confucius (Kong Qiu), the world-renowned Chinese philosopher born in Qufu, Shandong province, more than 2,500 years ago, has influenced Chinese society with his ideas right up to the present century. As the para-religious cult which came to embrace his thinking grew, shrines were

Colonnade in the Temple of Confucius

erected to his memory in Qufu. The feudal rulers of subsequent dynasties used Confucianism as a moral prop to consolidate their power, and built up the town of Qufu as if it were a Mecca. The result is a remarkable group of ancient buildings with art treasures.

Qufu has recently been restored to its former glory. It could well become a tourist attraction rivaling the Great Wall, which it pre-dates by a quarter-century.

In size and scale, this area ranks second only to the "Forbidden City" in Beijing. Construction of the Temple began in 478 B. C., the year after Confucius's death. It was rebuilt and enlarged many times during the ensuing 2,000 years.

The Temple grounds cover an area of 22 hectares with buildings laid out symmetrically along a 0.6-mile northsouth axis. There are 53 magnificent gateways and numerous halls, pavilions and shrines elaborately roofed with glazed tiles.

JIUHUASHAN MOUNTAIN

This mountain, in Qingyang county, Anhui province, stretches over an area of about 60 square miles. The mountain has a total of 99 peaks, among which the Shiwang is the highest, looming 4,398 ft. above sea level. Standing majestic, covered with jade-green vegetation, it is known in China as "the most picturesque mountain of the South-East".

The mountain was in the remote past known by another name—the Jiuzi Mountain. One day, as legend has it, Li Bai, a famous poet of the Tang Dynasty, contemplating its nine crests from the river below, thought they looked like lotus blossoms, and this inspired him to compose a verse: "From the azure skies above descends a jade-like flow, and nine fascinating lotuses rise out of the hills below". Hence the

Interior view of the Jiuhuashan Temple

Jiuzi Mountain was renamed Jiuhuashan, which means "the Mountain of the Nine Lotuses".

In the late eighth century, the mountain became a place where religious rites were held to worship the god of earth, and for centuries temples mushroomed there with incense smoke always filling the air. Thus it became famous as one of the four great Buddhist mountains in China (the other three being Emei Mountain in Sichuan province, Wutai Mountain in Shanxi province and the Putuo Mountain in Zhejiang province). There are still more than 50 well-preserved temples and over 6,000 sculptured Buddhas at Jiuhuashan. The most well-known temples include the Huachen Temple, the Qiyuan Temple, the Zhantanlin Temple, the Shangchan Hall, the Roushen Hall, the Baisui Temple, the Ganlu Temple, the Longchi Abbey, the Huiju Temple, the Gubaijing Altar and the Tiantai Temple. They contain many Buddhist relics.

NANJING

Nanjing, meaning "Southern Capital", is the capital of Jiangsu province. It is located on the east bank of the Yangtze River. It has been national capital several times in the past, and is today one of the most important national centers.

Nanjing is an attractive city, with wide, tree-lined boulevards and streets. To the west is the Yangtze, to the north the large Xuanwu Lake, and the east the Zijin, or Purple Mountains. Parts of the old walls of the town are still standing. They were constructed under the Ming in the late 14th century, and were originally 35 miles in perimeter with 13 gates. A number of the gates are also standing today.

It is clear from archaeological evidence that Nanjing has been inhabited since about 4000 B. C.

The settlement first became significant when it was a strategic part of the border between the three warring states, Wu, Yue, and Chu, over the period 467-221 B. C. Each king in turn adopted the town as his capital during the time he controlled it. When Qin Shi Huang unified the country in 221 B. C., Nanjing became a command post. Later, it developed into an important center under the Three Kingdoms.

During the Tang Dynasty, Nanjing again became an important center, and when this dynasty fell, it once again became the capital of a local dynasty known as the Southern Tang. Under the Southern Song, the town became an advance post in the war against the invaders from the north.

During the Ming Dynasty, Nanjing developed considerably, and was well known for shipbuilding, metal products, timber, and pottery. It also became an important cultural center. Students came from all over China to study at the Imperial College.

In all, Nanjing had been the capital of eight different

Sun Yat-sen Mausoleum

dynasties, from the third to the 15th century.

SUN YAT-SEN MAUSOLEUM

Nanjing houses the mausoleum of Dr. Sun Yat-Sen, leader of the 1911 revolution that overthrew the Qing Dynasty. He was buried there in 1929 on his own wishes. The mausoleum is on the southern slope of the Zijinshan in the eastern suburbs of Nanjing, and covers an area of 321 acres. From the entrance to the memorial hall there are 392 steps. At the center of the hall is a white marble statue of Dr. Sun Yat-Sen seated. In the vault where he is buried is a marble statue of Dr. Sun Yat-Sen in recumbent posture. the grounds are covered with pines, cypresses and fruit trees as well as trees sent in his honor from other countries.

ZIJINSHAN OBSERVATORY

Even if you are not interested in observatories, the trip to the one at Nanjing is worthwhile because you will be driven along narrow country lanes which eventually wind upwards through a thick green forest to a peak of Zijinshan, or the Purple and Gold Hills.

Outside the observatory proper is a collection of magnificent bronze castings of ancient astronomical instruments.

XUAN WU LAKE

One of Nanjing's scenic spots and a center for recreational and cultural activities, the lake is an extensive body of water with a circumference of 9.3 miles. It contains five islands linked by causeways and bridges. Before it was made into a public area in 1911, it had been the exclusive resort of the feudal aristocracy. Renovated and expanded after 1949, it is now six times its former size. The surrounding park includes a zoo, swimming pool, and theater.

TAIPING MUSEUM

The museum is located in the southern part of the town, housed in buildings which once formed part of the palace of

Xuan Wu Lake

the "Eastern King" under the Taiping "Celestial Emperor" Hong Xiuquan (1851-1864).

YUHUATAI (Rain of Flowers Terrace)

It is located in the southern area of the town, and derives its name from a legend about a monk who preached the tenets of Buddha so well that a rain of flowers fell upon his audience.

Throughout the centuries many temples have been built on the hill, but no trace of them remains. Several tombs have been unearthed there; there is also a modern stela erected in memory of the revolutionaries executed by the Kuomintang. Keep a lookout for pebbles when you visit this area: they are prized for their beauty. The pebbles can also be purchased from stalls in the grounds.

QUANZHOU

Quanzhou is situated on the bank of the Luoyang River south of Fuzhou, capital of Fujian province. It became a trading port in about the 6th century A. D. Towards the latter part of the Tang Dynasty, when the Perfume Route by Sea began to replace the overland Silk Road as China's link with the outside world, Quanzhou became one of the country's four major foreign trade ports. Ships leaving Quanzhou carried celebrated Chinese porcelain and silk fabrics to various parts of the world in exchange for perfumes, spices and precious stones. The city was enlarged during the Five-Dynasty period (10th century).

In 1974, a large wooden 12th or 13th century ship was discovered at the bottom of Quanzhou Bay. In it were found large quantities of perfume and spice from south-east Asia. The ill-fated ship was apparently just returning from a trip to the South Sea islands. The findings provided further proof that Quanzhou was, in the 12th or 13th century, already an important shipbuilding center and China's biggest seaport comparable to Alexandria in Egypt. The ship is now displayed in a special exhibition hall.

Marco Polo left his footprints in Quanzhou, and early Moslem missionaries visited the city.

As Quanzhou was once shaded by many coralbean trees, it came to be known to the outside world as the Coralbean City. Today, there are only a few of these trees left. Some line the road to the Kaiyuan Temple, one of the most interesting sites of this ancient port.

The temple, first constructed in the year 686. was originally named the Lotus Flower Temple. The site, according to legend, was once covered by a grove of mulberry trees. One day the owner of the trees dreamed that a Buddhist priest asked him for permission to build a temple here. Reluctant to do so, he said: "Only if the mulberry trees in my garden bear lotus flowers". A few days later, lotus flowers did blossom on his trees. Today in the courtyard west of the main hall, an ancient mulberry tree bears the sign: "Mulberry Lotus Tree".

The temple was later renamed several times until in 738, Tang Emperor Xuan Zong, a devout Buddhist, ordered every large town in China to name one of its temples "Kaiyuan", the title of his reign. The temple thus became known as Kaiyuan Temple.

Another interesting site is the Grand Mosque. Islam was introduced to China in 651., and from then on, many people from Arab countries came to Quanzhou on trade or religious missions. The local Moslems built a mosque in the year 1010. Also known as the Temple of the Unicorn, it is designed after the mosque in Damascus, and is one of the most famous Moslem buildings in China. Arabic inscriptions in the mosque record the year of its construction and its renovation in 1310 by Ahmad of Jerusalem.

Other places of interest in Quanzhou include Qingyuan and Jiuri Hills, Luoyang Bridge and the Holy Tombs.

*Pagoda of
the Yun
Yan Temple*

SUZHOU

Suzhou is located in the south of Jiangsu province, about 50 miles west of Shanghai, on the old Grand Canal. The city has been famous for its scenic beauty for many centuries. A Chinese proverb says: "In heaven there is paradise; on earth Suzhou and Hangzhou". The city has also long been noted for its beautiful women.

The city is situated on the delta plain of the Yangtze, an area dotted with lakes and ponds connected by a spider's web of, canals, and the roadways are linked by fine old humpbacked bridges. All the canals are lined with whitewashed houses with grey-tiled roofs.

The canals of the town eventually join up with the famous local waterway known as the Grand Canal, located to the west of the city. It is believed to be the largest internal waterway in the world, and was originally constructed to carry tribute grain from the Yangtze plain to the capital. Marco Polo, who visited Suzhou in the 13th century, wrote

81

that "the great Khan ... has made a huge canal of great width and depth from river to river and from lake to lake and made the water flow along it so that it looks like a big river ... By this means it is possible to go ... as far as Khan-balik" (the name for Beijing under the Yuan). Although the canal is not used for long-distance transport now, it is still heavily used by a great number of flat-bottomed boats under sail and engine power conveying agricultural produce to nearby towns.

Suzhou is one of the oldest towns in the Yangtze basin. It was founded in the fifth century B. C., when the King of Wu, He Lu, made it the capital of his Kingdom. The king is said to have been buried on Tiger Hill, a well-known landmark.

The town was given its present name in 589, under the Sui. It developed considerably under the Tang and Song. Indeed, it was under the Song, when Suzhou was about the same size as it is now but enclosed within walls, that some of the famous gardens were first established. And by then it had already become famous for silk weaving.

Many of the sites of the famous gardens of Suzhou, known as far back as the 10th century, are intact, and some have been restored to their former beauty. A visit to these gardens will be one of the highlights of your visit to China.

TIGER HILL

Tiger Hill, or Hu Qiu, a few miles north-west of the town, is very popular among visitors. It is supposedly the burial place of the King of Wu.

Two different reasons are given for the name of the hill. One is that the entrance gate resembles the mouth of a tiger, and the pagoda on the top of the hill its tail. The other is that when the King of Wu was buried on top of the hill, a tiger is said to have appeared there.

On top of this hill is an imposing structure—the pagoda of the Yun Yan (Cloud Rock) Temple built in 961. It is listed as one of the special historical sites under State protection. The temple courtyard is the highest point on the hill and commands a good view. The pagoda is one of the oldest in China, and has over the years developed a pronounced inclination.

COLD MOUNTAIN TEMPLE (Hanshansi)

It is located on the outskirts of town on a small canal crossed by an old humpbacked bridge. Green foliage hangs down over the saffron walls. When you visit this place you will understand why many poets have been inspired by the scenery there.

The temple's name comes from the hermit Han Shan, a Buddhist poet, sometime during the Tang Dynasty.

The temple owes its fame to the poem "Overnight Stay at Feng Qiao", by Zhang Ji, a Tang Dynasty poet.

PAGODAS

Suzhou has other pagodas, the most conspicuous being the twin pagodas of Two Pagoda Temple, or Shuangtasi. The temple no longer exists, and the site is now occupied by a school. Your guide may offer to take you to view the pagodas, which are accessible from a street called Dinghuisigang.

On the outskirts of town, in the south-west, you will find the pagoda of the Tample of Good Omen Light, or Ruiguangsita. The temple no longer exists, and only the seven-storey brick pagoda remains.

Another pagoda stands beside what was once the Temple Gratitude, or Paoensi, sometimes called the Northern Temple, or Bei Si. The temple was founded in the third century A. D., and has since been destroyed and rebuilt several times. All that now remains is the nine-storey pagoda thought to date from the 12th century.

Garden of the Master of Nets (Wangshi Yuan)

GARDENS

Suzhou is best-known for its landscaped gardens, over 150 in number. These are not large, but are fascinating in their delicate design, containing hills and ponds, terraces, corridors, towers, and almost everything that is needed in an "imperial garden". Of them, Liu Garden, which covers about 10 acres, is the largest in Suzhou, and certainly one of the most attractive. It was one of the few gardens that escaped destruction during the Taiping rebellion in the middle of the 19th century, and this is symbolized in its name, the Chinese character for which means "to keep".

The garden was first laid out during the Ming Dynasty by a civil servant who also had the West Garden, or Xi Yuan, constructed.

You will find a series of small lakes linked by bridges and numerous buildings, of which the most interesting is the Hall of the Mandarin Ducks (symbols of love). Others have windows offering good views of the landscape. You should also take time to visit the section of the garden planted with fruit trees. Ask your guide to take you to the section devoted to the cultivation of miniature trees. There are hundreds of them; one pomegranate tree is more than 200 years old. In this section you will also see numerous trays containing miniature landscapes and rockeries. The owners and residents of the private gardens in ancient China preferred not to leave their beautiful surroundings, and therefore had miniature landscapes made to remind them of other beauty spots.

WUXI

Wuxi is an important town in Jiangsu province. While the town itself has few buildings or sites of historic or archaeological interest, it nevertheless is an attractive place to visit with its network of canals and cobbled streets. The major attraction for most visitors is Tai Lake, a few miles to the south.

Foreign tourists cruising on a pleasure-boat on the Grand Canal

Wuxi is an old city, founded 2,000 years ago under the Han (206 B. C.-221 A. D.). It remained a small settlement until the sixth century, when some development took place as a result of the construction of the Grand Canal. The canal passes right through the center of Wuxi.

Over the centuries that followed, Wuxi remained a small country town, and it was not until the 13th century that economic expansion took place. In the 1930s, local and foreign investment led to the establishment of numerous factories producing silk, cotton, vegetable oils, and flour. It also became a central market for crops and agricultural produce destined for nearby Shanghai.

Following the 1949 revolution, Wuxi was further industrialized, with particular emphasis placed on the machine-building and machine-tool industry.

LAKE TAIHU

Since the days of ancient China, the fascinating beauty of Lake Taihu has attracted poets, painters, scholars and eminent people.

Spring in Tai Lake

One of China's five major freshwater lakes, Taihu covers an area of 1,500 square miles. As a natural reservoir, it supplies life-giving water to vast tracts of land.

For anyone who loves the sea, the vastness of Lake Taihu has a special appeal—from any one point some other portion of shoreline is out of sight. The lake contains three islets joined together, forming a contour that resembles a turtle.

By the lakeside are Meiyuan (Plum Garden), Liyuan (Li Garden) and Yuantouzhu (Tortoise Head Garden), each known for its unique beauty and history. Of the three, Yuantouzhu is the largest. Extending into the lake like a tortoise frolicking in the water, it offers the best view of the lake. On a misty day, it is particularly enchanting. With the fog-covered Turtle Islets in the distance and a fishing boat gliding past, it is a scene straight out of a traditional landscape painting.

WUYI MOUNTAIN

Aquiline rock on the Wuyi Mountain

Wuyi Mountain, in south-east China's Fujian province, on the border with Jiangxi, is in fact a series of red sandstone hills covering about 30 square miles. It is one of China's best-known beauty spots.

A green river weaves its way around the red hills. Two of the best sites are of the "Three-Three" and the "Six-Six". The former is the river, which bends nine times as it meanders around the foot of the mountain, and the latter refers to the 36 peaks rising steeply from the river. For more than 1,000 years, poets have flocked there to write praises of its natural beauty.

The area is said to combine the awe of Huangshan Mountain, the elegance of the Guilin peaks and the grandeur

Sunrise on the Grand Canal

of Mount Tai. Apart from its scenery, the Wuyi Mountain area contains many historical relics, such as the "Boat Coffins in Cliff Caves". From the Qin and Han dynasties, Taoists and necromancers visited the area to preach their doctrines. More than 300 monasteries, towers and pavilions were built, and over 700 inscriptions carved into the red rocks.

YANGZHOU

Yangzhou, a city in Jiangsu province, is located on the lower reaches of the Yangtze River and the Huaihe River. It has a history dating back to 486 B. C., when a long ditch called the Han Ditch was dug. This project later led to the

Jianzhen Statue in Daming Temple

construction of the Grand Canal that stretched over 1,000 miles to link the fertile south with Beijing.

Yangzhou was a major ancient economic and cultural center in eastern China.

The famous monk, Jianzhen, sailed from there to take Buddhist doctrine to Japan during the Tang Dynasty. Puhaddin, a 16th-generation descendant of the prophet, Mohammed, came to Yangzhou on a religious mission in the 13th century, and was buried on his own wish in the city. Marco Polo served as the city's governer general for three years, and left footprints all over the city.

Yangzhou has many historical sites. Among them are the 1,500-year-old Daming Temple, the Fajin Temple built partly to commemorate the monk, Jianzhen, and ruins of temporary palaces that used by several emperors for some 2,000 years.

The most interesting scenic spot in the city perhaps is Shou Xihu, or Slim West Lake, which is so named because it resembles the West Lake in Hangzhou in terms of natural beauty, but is narrower and more twisted.

Slim West Lake

Mountain Resort in Chengde

CHENGDE

Tucked away in a valley 155 miles northeast of Beijing, the mountain resort at Chengde, formerly known as the Jehol Summer Palace, is one of the biggest and most celebrated former imperial gardens in China.

Opened in recent years to foreign tourists, the imperial garden is far less well-known than Beijing's Fobidden City or Summer Palace — despite the fact that it is bigger than both of them combined, 2.16 sq. miles to be precise.

It is the natural beauty of Chengde, plus its pleasantly cool climate even at the height of summer, that caught the fancy of the second emperor of the Qing Dynasty, Kangxi, when he toured the region in the early days of his reign.

Park-laying and palace construction started in 1703, and the resort reached its present dimensions in 1970.

With four clusters of magnificent halls, palaces and pavilions nesting among the wooded slopes inside a meandering, six-mile, red-painted wall, the area is a superb blend of traditional architecture and landscape gardening, mixing the courtyard styles typical of north China with the soft, misty landscapes of the south.

Qing emperors regularly spent several summer months at the resort, and it was there that Emperor Qian Long received an emissary from England—the first Western envoy to visit the Qing court.

Outside the palace wall are the "Eight Outer Temples" built to celebrate birthdays of emperors and their mothers. They include elements of Han, Tibetan and Mongolian architecture. One is a replica of the Potala Palace at Lhasa in Tibet, and another houses a giant standing Buddha statue 70 ft. tall.

DATONG

Among the unsung wonders of China's history-soaked heritage are the 1,500-year-old Buddhist grottoes of Datong—an eight-hour train journey from Beijing—in Shanxi province.

In a valley at Yungang, some 10 miles west of Datong and easily reached by taxi or public bus, more than 50 recesses have been dug into the hills and filled with every size and type of Buddhist statue imaginable — 51,000 altogether.

From the 56 ft. Seated Buddha to tiny figures just a few centimeters high, every wall and archway is crammed with carvings, including serial-type representations of scenes from Buddhist mythology and the lives of famous monks.

Datong has several other tourist attractions—such as the 600-year-old Nine Dragon Screen made of glazed tiles,

Yungang Grottos

the Huayan Monastery with the largest wooden shrine hall in China, and the Shanhua Monastery, intact since 713

HOHHOT

If you are tired of the romantic portrayal of cowboy lifestyle presented in westerns, and want to get a real taste of the vast prairie and nomadic life, Hohhot is an ideal place to go.

Located to the north of Beijing, near the border with the People's Republic of Mongolia, Hohhot is the capital of China's Inner Mongolia Autonomous Region, an area characterized by vast expanses of grassland and desert. The city of Hohhot, as legend has it, was built over 400 years ago by a clan of Mongols, whose chief was a descendant of Genghis Khan. As the construction was supervised by a woman named "San Niangzi", it was originally called "San Niangzi City". Later, it was formally named Hohhot, meaning "Green City", because it looked like a raised green

Tomb of Wang Zhaojun

oasis when viewed from afar. Some say that the name is derived from the green tomb of Wang Zhaojun, a beautiful imperial concubine who crossed the desert 2,000 years ago to marry a minority chief in an effort to secure peace between the Han Dynasty and the native Xiongnus. In this "Green City", Emperess Dowager Ci Xi of the late Qing Dynasty was born and grew up.

Apart from the tomb of Wang Zhaojun, Hohhot has several tourist attractions — such as the Five Pagoda Temple faced with beautifully-carved glazed bricks, the Wanbuhuayanjing Pagoda, the base facades of which are considered masterpieces of Liao Dynasty sculpture in the 10th-century A.D., and the Drum Tower, or Gu Lou, built as part of the Great Wall under the Qing.

But the most exciting tourist attractions are probably the yurt camp and Nadam Fair.

Yurt Camp: a pleasant excursion that will take you back hundreds of years to nomadic life is to Wulantuge, 54 miles north of Hohhot. There you can wear Mongolian costume, ride nimble Mongolian ponies or huge bactrian camels and graze "your cattle" on the fertile grassland. Or you can just take a bow and go "hunting" for your family. After a day's work, you can retreat to your warm and cozy yurt and be treated to a rich dinner — savoury milk-tea and sesame pancakes, roast leg of lamb or whole lamb, or braised ox-tail. In the evening, you can sit with your hosts around a campfire or listen to the music from a horse-head violin-type instrument called a matouqin. Apart from Wulantuge, there are two other yurt camps, at Huitengxile, 180 miles from Hohhot and Baiyunheshao, 107 miles away. Altogether, there are more than 50 yurts and a restaurant specially set up in these pastoral areas to cater for tourists.

Nive Pagoda Temple

Nadam Fair: if your trip to Inner Mongolia conincides with the annual Nadam Fair held in the autumn, you will have a chance to feast your eyes on this nine-day colorful festival of the Mongolian ethnic group. Nadam, meaning "games", is a traditional Mongolian gala based on the recreational and martial activities of horse racing, archery and wrestling. In the era of the Xiongnus nearly 2,000 years ago, these three games were very popular. From the Jin Dynasty (1115-1234 A.D.), they combined to become a regular gala, in which winners in the three events were awarded prizes. And the venue was usually a piece of uninhabited grassland which would suddenly became a town as yurts mushroomed seemingly overnight. Today, Nadam serves not only as an annual sports tournament but also a grand trade fair.

Yurt camp for tourists

TAIYUAN

Taiyuan, the capital of Shanxi (meaning "West of the Mountains") province, has probably seen more violence in its thousands of years of existence than any other city in China.

Situated at the northern end of the Loess Plateau and looking down on the vast north China plain to the east, Taiyuan — originally called Jinyang and built in 497 B.C. — was an important strategic fort for many turbulent centuries. Despite elaborate precautions taken to prevent invasions from the northern steppes, minority troops took the town on a number of occasions and settled in the region.

Wars and fires have ruined Jinyang several times. during the Tang Dynasty, a fierce battle was fought around Jinyang, and when it fell, the great dynasty fell with it. It was again destroyed by war in 979, and had to be rebuilt in 982 on the site of a town called Tangming north of Jinyang. it was then named Taiyuan.

Taiyuan's tourist attractions include the Twin Pagodas Monastery, more than 160 ft. high, which forms the city's emblem, Chongshan Monastery, with a rich collection of Buddhist sutras, Xuanzhong Monastery, an ancient temple where the Japanese Pure Land Buddhist sect originated, and Shuanglin Monastery, which is known as the treasure house of oriental sculpture art.

Some 16 miles west of Taiyuan stands a temple calld Jinci, one of the province's most famous. Built during the Northern Wei Dynasty (386-534 A.D.), the temple was originally a place for worshiping ancestors, but over the centuries it became a retreat of emperors and princes. It is still surrounded by cypresses and natural springs.

To the north is the famous Mount Wutai, one of China's four Buddhist shrines. Wutai, meaning five

Statues of maidservants of the Song Dynasty in the Jinci Temple

platforms, consists of five platform-shaped and finger-like peaks. The first Tafu Temple of Divine Vulture built more than 1,900 years ago. At one time, there were more than 200 temples tiered up along the slopes, attracting thousands of monks and worshippers from all over the country. The ravages of war, weather and neglect over the years, however, ruined many of the temples and reduced their number to a few dozen. Careful restoration work has been carried out for years in a bid to restore the cluster of temples to their former grandeur.

The jingle of hundreds of bells can be heard from an enormous white dagoba at the foot of Wutai. This, together with the coiling incense smoke, adds to the atmosphere of a long lost holy land.

CHANGCHUN

Changchun, the capital of Jilin province, is a Chinese version of a combination of Detroit and Hollywood. it has China's largest motor vehicle plant and its biggest film studio.

Located in the center of the northeast plain, Changchun, meaning "eternal spring", was first settled more than 1,000 years ago. But it did not develop much until the turn of this century. The city grew enormously in the 1930s after it was made the capital of the Japanese puppet state, Manchukuo, during the Japan's military occupation of the area (1931-1945).

The city has been developed rapidly since the founding of the People's republic in 1949, and has become a major industrial and cultural city. It has few historical sites or

Women of Korean nationality in Northeast China performing "Springboard" jumping

ancient monuments to offer tourists. But if you are interested in how cars and trucks are made in China, then you can visit the No. 1 Automobile Plant. If film-making interests you, you can arrange a tour of the Changchun Film Studio, the same way you visit the Universal Studio at Hollywood.

The only major historical site you can visit is the imperial palace of China's last emperor, in northeast Changchun. The palace covers an area of 127,000 square yards. It is nothing like the imperial palaces in Beijing or Shenyang. Most of it is comprised of simple houses, and the lay-out is crude, all reflecting the hasty establishment of the Japanese puppet state, headed by Puyi, China's last emperor dethroned in the 1911 revolution.

HARBIN

Harbin is the capital of Heilongjiang, China's northernmost province, which borders the Soviet Union. Situated in the middle reaches of the Songhua River, it is a busy river port. Several roads and railways converge at Harbin, so it is also an important communications hub.

Harbin used to be a fishing village, and its name, in Manchu dialect, means drying fishnets. Unlike most provincial capitals in China, it has a very short history. Harbin was incorporated as a town in 1898. Since the founding of the People's Republic in 1949 it has rapidly evolved into an industrial city. Today you will find factories engaged in the production of motor vehicles and related products, as well as its processing plants for tobacco and grain.

The Songhua flows through the city from west to east, providing an ideal place for summer swimming.

Winter is cold and long there, usually lasting seven months from october to April. The long winter gives birth to the famous art of ice sculpture.

Sun Island Resort

The Sun Island is one of northern China's most scenic spots and is famous throughout the country as a resort. The island is in the Songhua River, and contains many sanatoriums, villas, pavilions and kiosks surrounded by trees and flower beds.

HUNTING GAMES AT TAOSHAN

The hunting Ground at Taoshan (Peach Mountains) is China's first hunting ground opened to foreign tourists. Located at the western foot of the Lesser Xing'an Mountains, it covers more than 49, 410 acres of vast virgin forest, and is only a four-hour train ride north of Harbin.

Game includes bears, red deer, wild boar, roe deer, wild goats, lynx, otters, weasels, snow rabbits and squirrels.

101

Ice-carvings shows

ICE-CARVINGS SHOWS

These are held in Zhaolin Park in January and February every year. Ice-carvings of a great variety are displayed. In the evening, the whole park is lit with lanterns, and the glittering ice-sculptures turn it into a shining crystal palace.

SHENYANG

Shenyang is the capital of Liaoning province, about 500 miles north of Beijing. The city used to be known as Mukden, a name used by the Tartar people who once ruled the area. It has a history of more than 2,000 years, but it did not rise to prominence until it became the Qing capital between 1625 and 1644. When the Qing took Beijing in 1644 and established a dynasty based there, Mukden became its secondary capital and remained so far 250 years.

Now Shenyang is one of China's major industrial centers thanks to the rich deposits of coal, iron ore and nonferrous ore throughout Liaoning province.

The Imperial Palace there is now a museum, displaying historical artifacts of the Qing Dynasty. At one time it served as the Imperial Palace of emperors Nu Er Ha Chi and Huang Tai Ji.

It covers an area of 15 acres, with 300 rooms in 70 buildings, dispersed in a dozen courtyards. it is the best preserved cluster of imperial structures in the country next only to the Forbidden City in Beijing. Resembling the latter in style and lay-out, it is characterized by the blend architecture of Man and Han nationalities.

The Bei Ling (Nothern Imperial Tomb), north of Shenyang, was built in 1643. Covering 1,112 acres, it is where Emperor Shun Zhi's father, Huang Tai Ji, and mother, Bo Er Ji Ji, were buried. Once the exclusive domain of the Imperial family of the Qing Dynasty, it is now a magnificent public park, open to all for rest and recreation.

To the east, the Dong Ling (Eastern Imperial Tomb) is where the first emperor of the Qing Dynasty, Nu Er Ha Chi, and his wife were buried. The grounds are pleasant and attractive, with flowers, shrubs, and many ancient trees.

Imperial Palace in Shenyang

DUNHUANG

A 27-hour journey northwest from Lanzhou by train and then by bus will take you to Dunhuang, Gansu province, the outpost on the "Silk Road", known as Shazhou in the distant past.

As a prefecture it was first set up in the 13th year of the reign of Emperor Wu of the Han Dynasty (111 B.C.). A

At the foot of the Mogao Grottos

gateway to the Western Regions, it served as a pivotal point of cultural and trade interchange during the Han and Tang dynasties. Caravans, their pack animals loaded with exquisite silk products, travelled past it from the ancient capital, Changan. On reaching Dunhuang, the travellers would separate and proceed along two different routes in their westward journey. The northern route, starting from the Yumen Pass, reached out to the west via Turpan and Kuqa, while the southern route, starting from the Yangguan Pass, stretched westward through the Luobu Lake. Dunhuang was the first stopover too, for incoming traffic by way of the two passes, bringing in the Dawan horses, grapes and clover, as well as Buddhist sutras from India.

The Yumen Pass, the former terminal pass of the Great Wall, popularly known as "Square Town", is situated by a lake over 50 miles to the northwest of Dunhuang. It is called YU-MEN, or "Jade Gate", because the Khotian jade used to be carried to the interior through this strategic point. Yangguan, or "Sunshine Pass", located to the east of the South Lake, 44 miles south of Dunhuang, is said to be well-blessed with sunshine.

The famous Mogao Grottoes are situated in a valley 16 miles southeast of Dunhuang. These were first hewed out in 366. Additions and repairs, made in the 1,000 years from the Northern Wei to the Yuan dynasties, resulted in a honeycomb of grottoes representing different artistic styles of different times. The most artistic are probably those dating from the Tang Dynasty. Today, a total of 492 caves are still in good condition, with 54,000 square yards of murals, more than 2,000 painted statues, and five wooden buildings constructed in the Tang and Song dynasties. The Mogao Grottoes are among the oldest of their kind in China.

Jiayuguan

JIUQUAN

The next major stopover on the "Silk Road" northwestwards from Lanzhou, is Jiuquan, a town named after its "wine spring".

From the second century B.C., commissioners and high-ranking officers were dispatched by the rulers of the Western Han Dynasty (206 B.C.-24 A.D.) to develop the region. As the traffic along the "Silk Road" became busier and more important, the prefecture of Jiuquan was established, more than 1,600 years ago, to protect this vital artery. On a triumphant expedition, as legend has it, Huo Qubing, a celebrated commander of the Western Han army, visited the town with his troops. Emperor Wudi had decreed that they should feast on wine, but there was not enough to go round, so Huo poured his cup of wine into a spring so that it could be "shared" with his soldiers. Hence the name.

The city's Drum Tower, erected in 343, used to be called

"Night Watchman's Tower" on the east city gate. As the city expanded, it was edged into the inner city and its name was changed to "Drum Tower." It is the only remaining structure there of the many Marco Polo praised in his writings.

A few miles away from the city is the Jiayuguan Pass, at the western end of the Great Wall. The Great Wall used to end at Yumen (about 50 miles to the west of Jiayuguan) before the pass was abandoned during the Ming Dynasty. The walls in the northwest region were originally constructed under the Han, and remains of the Han wall have been found near Dunhuang, but the portions of the wall standing at Jiayuguan date from the early Ming, and are about six centuries old. You can stand on the terrace of the gate tower and look back at the wall winding its way along the mountain ridges. To the south are the snow-capped Qilian Mountains, and to the west, the desert.

In a tomb chamber at Dingjiazha, Jiuquan, are some of the country's earliest murals, dating back to the East Jin Dynasty (317-420 A.D.).

LANZHOU

Lanzhou, the capital of Gansu province, is an important stop on your journey along the ancient "Silk Road" west from Xi'an.

Situated on the upper reaches of the Yellow River, Lanzhou has been important for thousands of years because of the Hexi Corridor, or "Corridor West of the Yellow River", in which early Chinese civilizaton began. About 3,000 years ago, in the Zhou Dynasty, agriculture began to take shape in the basins of the Jin and Wei rivers which formed the corridor, marking the beginning of the great Yellow River basin civilization.

Starting in the Qin Dynasty, merchants and traders

travelling from Xi'an to central Asia and then on to the Roman Empire, or the other way round, broke their long journey at Lanzhou. To protect this corridor and important communications hub, the Great Wall was extended under the Han as far as Yumen, in the far northwest of present-day Gansu province.

Lanzhou became capital of a succession of tribal states during the turbulent centuries that followed the decline of the Han. However, during this time of turmoil, people began to be attracted to ideologies that satisfied their need for hope. Taoism developed into a religion, and Buddhism became the official religion in some of the northern states. Buddhist religious art also flourished, and shrines were built in temples, caves, and on cliffs. From the fifth to the 11th centuries, Dunhuang, beyond the Yumen Pass of the Great Wall, became a center for Budhist study, drawing scholars and pilgrims from afar. It was a period in which magnificent works of art were created.

The first great iron bridge on the Yellow River

Delicious Bai Lan melon

URUMQI

The last stopover on your westward journey along the "Silk Road" is Urumqi, the capital of the Xinjiang Uygur Autonomous Region, situated at the northern foot of the snow-capped Tianshan Mountains.

Urumqi, meaning "fine pasture" in Mongolian, was inhabited by a mixture of ethnic groups nearly 2,000 years ago. Because the northern route of the "Silk Road" passed through it, it became a heavily-guarded fort in the Han Dynasty, and remained so for centuries. But today, the city itself has few historical sites to offer tourists, except for the museum of the autonomous region that houses some valuable relics unearthed along the "Silk Road". An excursion to Tianchi, however, is worthwhile.

Tianchi, or "Lake of Heaven", is about 30 miles southeast of Urumqi, at an elevation of 6,435 ft. above sea level. It is a beautiful highland lake, flanked by rugged pines and cypresses, and with clear waters that reflect the surrounding mountains. In winter, it provides an ideal alpine

109

Lake of Heaven, the gem of Tianshan Mountains.

skating rink. In fact, China's winter skating games have been held there.

A 112-mile journey southeast from Urumqi will take you to the oasis of Turpan, which lies in one of the world's great land depressions, 505 feet below sea level. Known as a "Furnace Town", its summer temperature soars regularly into the 100s Fahrenheit, while the desert rocks are said to reach 170°F. But it is well irrigated and produces much fruit such as seedless grapes and Hami melons.

To the southeast of Turpan can be seen the ruins of Gaochang, once a thriving town in the first century B.C., standing against a background of arid mountains which look like giant ant hills.

Donkey-drawn cart in the Gobi desert of Xinjiang

XI'AN

Xi'an was one of the most important cradles of Chinese civilization. It marked the start of the famous "Silk Road" that linked China with central Asia and the Roman Empire. And it served as the first capital of a unified China and capital of 11 dynasties periodically from the 11th century B.C. to the early 10th century A.D.

Xi'an, or Changan as it was called in ancient times, is known as the city of "Everlasting Peace", which should definitely not be missed on your journey through China.

Located between rivers and mountains in the center of the fertile Guanzhong Plain in Shaanxi province, Xi'an — the provincial capital — is the natural place to nurture the nation's civilization. Back in the Neolithic Age, about 6,000 years ago, as excavations show, a matriarchal clan was formed at Banpo village in the region.

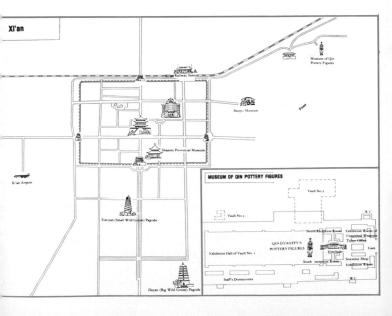

Thousands of years later, the Zhou kings established their capital in settlements only a few miles from the present-day city. In 221 B.C., Qin Shi Huang, the first emperor of unified China, set about enlarging the settlement of Xianyang, about 15 miles northwest of the city. This town, established under earlier Qin rulers as the capital, became heavily populated, so that in 212 B.C., Qin Shi Huang decided to move his court to the south bank of the Wei River. A vast palace was begun. However, work was never completed in his lifetime, and some years later when the Qin fell to the Han (206 B.C.), this and most of the other palaces were destroyed.

The conqueror, Liu Bang, first emperor of the Han Dynasty, also estblished the site of his capital only a few miles north of modern Xi'an.

From about 25 A.D., the town went into a decline that lasted about five and a half centuries, until, in 582 A.D., the Sui emperor, Wen Di, established his capital southeast of Changan. The place flourished and developed so quickly under the Tang Dynasty that in time it became the most important city in Asia, with a population of about a million people living in a vast, well-planned area protected by large walls with ramparts. The area occupied by the old city was greater than that of present-day Xi'an.

For over a millennium from the Second Century B.C., China's silk was transported from Xi'an to central Asia and Europe. Although damaged by several wars, Xi'an, covering 880 square miles and with a population of 2,915,000 still contains a host of historical sites.

SHAANXI PROVINCIAL
MUSEUM (Forest of Stele)

The Shaanxi Provincial Museum is an enlargement of the Forest of Stele, which is located on the site of the ancestral temple of the Tang Dynasty. The garden-type museum of ancient architecture is mainly for the protection of cultural relics and the display and study of antiquities. The Forest of Stele was first founded in 1090 A.D. during the Song Dynasty. It is the oldest and richest collection of stele in China. The stele are numerous enough to be likened to a forest, hence the name. This fordst consists of six large exhibition halls, seven corridors and a stele pavilion. There are more than 1,000 stele of eight dynasties from the Han down to the Qing. They are of great value to historians and for the study of calligraphic development.

MAUSOLEUM OF QIN SHI HUANG AND MUSEUM OF THE QIN TERRACOTTA FIGURES

Qin Shi Huang (259-210 B.C.), was the founding emperor of the Qin Dynasty. His tomb is on the south bank of the Wei River, about three miles east of the county town of Lintong. It is one of China's most important historical sites.

Built in 247 B.C., when Qin Shi Huang was enthrouned

Terracotta figures of armed warriors and horses

at the age of 13, the mausoleum is in fact a deep and magnificent underground palace. According to records, more than 700,000 people were employed to construct it, and the work took 36 years. The inner conditions of the mausoleum remain unknown because it has not yet been excavated.

In 1974 and 1976, three massive army vaults were discovered. In Vault No. 1, the largest, 6,000 life-size terracotta figures of armed warriors and horses were buried. An underground feat of civil engineering, Vault No. 1 is 251 yards long from east to west, 68 yards wide from north to south, and 5.47 yards deep, covering an area of 15,601 sq. yd. The three army vaults were ascertained by archaeologists to be pits for burial objects accompanying the tomb of Qin Shi Huang. In October, 1979, an on-site museum was built above Vault No. 1.

Ranging from 5.8 to 6 ft. in height, the vivid life-size warrior figures are clad in armour or short gowns belted at the waist, with leggings and tightly-lashed boots, and holding real weapons — bows and arrowa, swords and spears.

BIG GOOSE PAGODA

Located a couple of miles south of Xi'an city, the Big Goose Pagoda, the city's emblem, was first built in 652 A.D., as part of the Ci'en Temple, which was constructed in 648 on the order of Crown Prince Li Zhi (later Emperor Gao Zong) of the Tang Dynasty in memory of his mother Empress Wende. The Venerable Xuan Zang, a renowned monk returned from a pilgrimage to India and neighboring countries, proposed that the pagoda should be built to store the Buddhist scriptures he had brought back. Xuan Zang was made abbot of the temple, where he translated the scriptures into Chinese. From 701 to 704, the five-storey pagoda was rebuilt into a seven-storey structure 221 ft. high

*Small Goose
Pagoda*

with stairs winding up to the top floor. Built with grey bricks,
this pavilion-like pagoda with arched portals on each floor is
a masterpiece of Buddhist architecture with a distinct
Chinese style.

SMALL GOOSE PAGODA

This temple is near the Big Goose Pagoda, and was built
in 707 A.D. It has 15 storeys and is 148 ft. high. It has a fine
and delicate style. On the north and south doors are
exquisitely-carved ivory designs and Buddhist figures.

BANPO MUSEUM

This neolithic site is a few miles from Xi'an. The Banpo
people settled here some 6,000 years ago. They cultivated
their land, built houses, and lived as primitive clan. Five
excavations since 1954 have uncovered a village of 45
houses, Stone Age pottery, tools, and bones. The site covers
an area of 60,000 sq. yd. It is divided into living quarters, a

115

pottery-making center and a graveyard. The museum built to protect the site has a hall covering 23,400 sq. ft. and two exhibition rooms.

HUAQING HOT SPRING

This natural hot spring is located at the foot of Mt. Lishan, a scenic spot 18 miles east of Xi'an.

According to historical records, hot springs were found here 2,800 years ago. A palace called "Li Gong" was built here during the Western Zhou Dynasty. A hot spring bath was constructed for the royal family during the Qin Dynasty. It was extended on several occasions during the Han and Tang dynastis. A larger palace called Hua Qing was built on the mountain side in 747 A.D. The hot spring bath can hold 400 people at one time. Flowing at a rate of 110 tons per hour from four different sources, the water, with a temperature of 109 degrees Fahrenheit, contains nine minerals, such as lime and manganese carbonate, which are said to be efficacious in soothing skin and rheumatoid ailments.

Huaqing Hot Spring Pool

Xining, the capital of Qinghai province, used to be a major stop on the Silk Road's southern route.

It is one of the poorest provincial capitals in China, and has little of real interest to offer a tourist. But some worthwhile excursions begin there.

TA'ER TEMPLE

Ta'er Temple, also known as the "Pagoda Lamasery", is one of China's largest Buddhist temples, and a sacred place of the "Yellow Sect of Tibetan Lamaism". Located in Lushaer, to the southwest of Xining, the temple is still used for worship by "Yellow Sect" believers.

Lamaism took root in Tibet in the seventh century A.D. as a new form of Buddhism. Over the centuries that followed, numerous sects developed. In the 15th century, a well-known Lama called Zongkaba founded a new reformed sect, which strictly observed Buddhist precepts. His

Sites in ancient town on the once important "Silk Road".

Ta'er Temple, one of China's largest lamaseries

followers were easily indentified by their hats, hence the derivation of the name "Yellow (Hat) Sect". Their influence increased to such an extent that they eventually became the ruling sect in Tibet. They were also granted the patronage of the Ming and Qing courts, who built a grand "Yellow Sect" lamasery called "Yong He Palace" in Beijing.

Since Zongkaba was born in Lushaer, a number of pagodas were built there to know him. Then, in 1560, a small lamasery was built to enclose them, and this was enlarged over the centuries into a magnificent lamasery, which ranks closely in importance with the Dazhao Lamasery at Lhasa. There are numerous prayer halls, pagodas and priceless works of art such as sutras, porcelain from the 13th century, magnificent collections of embossed embroideries, carpets and superb statues.

118

CHENGDU

Chengdu, the capital of Sichuan province, has been the economic and cultural heart of China's most-populous region since 400 B.C.

During the Eastern Han Dynasty (25-220 A.D.), the imperial court appointed an official to supervise the fast-growing brocade industry in the town. Thus it became known as Jincheng, or Brocade Town. When it was discovered that the brocade turned brighter and fresher after being washed in the nearby river, it was given the name Jin Jiang, or Brocade River.

During the Five Dynasties era (907-960 A.D.), it was for a time the capital of China, and hibiscus was planted all along the city wall. Because of this, it then became known as the City of Furong or Hibiscus. Today, flowers and trees grace the wide streets and the many parks. Agriculture and light industry are the dominant mainstays of the region. Brocade is still manufactured along with other textiles and handicrafts. If you stay in Chengdu, you may be able to see an operatic production. The Sichuan Opera has been in existence for many years and is slowly winning nationwide fame.

Places of interest in the city include Du Fu Caotang, a small thatched hut in which the great poet, Du Fu, of the Tang Dynasty wrote many of his 240-odd poems.

But the more exciting sights can be seen on the excursions to Mt. Emei, the Great Buddha Statue at Leshan, the Thousand Buddha Cliffs at Guangyuan and the Guanxian Dam.

MOUNT EMEI

Mount Emei rises sharply on the left bank of the Dadu

The top of Mount Emei wrapped in mist and cloud

River 125 miles south from Chengdu by road. Reaching a height of. 10,227 ft. it is the highest of the four sacred Buddhist mountains in China. There were once over 70

temples and monasteries that sheltered thousands of Buddhist monks. Pilgrims spent days climbing to the top of Mount Emei to offer prayers to the Buddha. Most of the temples still remain, and you can see them on your climb to the summit. The climb is tiring and the path difficult to follow in places. At the summit you may see the sun rise over the famous Ocean of Clouds. Late in the afternoon, you may also be fortunate enough to see the Precious Light of Buddha formed by the diffraction of light passing through moisture particles in the atmosphere.

GREAT BUDDHA STATUE AT LESHAN

Leshan, about 100 miles southwest of Chengdu, once known as Jiading or Jiazhou, is a 1,300-year-old city in

Great Buddha Statue at Leshan

Joy with monkeys on the Mount Emei

southwestern Sichuan province, where the Minjiang River and the Dadu River converge. It is a junction for land and water traffic in southern Sichuan.

On Lingyun Hill, an enormous Buddha, 231 ft. tall, sits erect with an armed guard standing at either side. It is carved into a cliff overlooking three rivers. To the left, a path with nine bends winds down the cliff from the top of the Buddha's head, at the crest of the hill, to the statue's feet. Legend has it the Monk Hai Tong of Lingyun Monastery, disturbed at seeing many boats capsized in the tubulent waters nearby, initiated the carving of this Buddha to subdue the waters and ensure the safety of the river folk. It was completed in 803, under the Tang Dynasty, after 90 years of work. The figure, not only a great work of art, incorporates the sophisticated technical features of hidden drains which have been skillfully cut through the body to prevent the surface from weathering.

THOUSAND BUDDHA CLIFFS
AT GUANGYUAN

The Famous Thousand Buddha Cliffs at Guangyuan

Treasure Bottle Mouth, an integrating part of the ancient Guanxian Dam water systems.

If you are traveling from Chengdu to Xi'an by rail and are interested in Buddhist cave sculptures, it is worth stopping at Guangyuan. It is located about 175 miles north of Chengdu in the north of the province, only 30 miles from the Shaanxi border. Not far from the town is the Thousand Buddha Cliffs, or Qian Fo Yan, where there are Buddhist sculptures comparable with those at Yungang (see Datong) and Long Men (see Luoyang). The carvings were begun in the early part of the eighth century, but of the original 17,000 statues, only a few hundred remain.

THE GUANXIAN DAM

This dam is located about 30 miles to the northwest of Chengdu. The Minjiang River splits into four tributaries near the town, two of which flow on either side of Chengdu.

Over the centuries, a series of water systems has been developed at Guanxian, th first as far back as 250 B.C. The water has been diverted from the Minjiang to the nearby plains, creating one of the most productive agricultural areas in the whole of China.

There are models at the dam site that illustrate the water systems, as well as inscriptions commemorating the scholar, Li Bing and his son, who began the task of diverting the waters more than 22 centuries ago.

Nearby is a Taoist temple, the Fulongguan, commanding a superb view of the river valley. A short drive away stands the Two Kings' Temple, built in honor of Li Bing and his son, who were both awarded the title of "King" after their deaths.

CHONGQING

Chongqing stands on a magnificent site — a high promontory overlooking the confluence of the Yangtze and Jialing rivers. From the pine-clad hills surounding the town, mists sweep down and cloak the rickety wooden houses to the treacherous river.

While there, you must make sure to visit Chao Tian Men, or the Gate to the Sky. From this spot there is a superb view of the river far below. Another beauty spot is Nanbei, or Southern Hot Springs, about 12 miles from the city on the right bank of the Jialing River. The area has natural caves, small lakes and pleasant parks, as does the South Mountain Gardens, or Nanshan Gongyuan.

If you still have time, try to visit the site of the Buddhist carvings near Dazu, about 125 miles from Chongqing by road. The carvings are over 1,100 years old, and, although not as widely known as those at Dunhuang, Long Men, and Yungang, are splendid works of Buddhist religious art. There are 13 sites, the most important being Beishan, Baoding, Qianfoyan, and Miaogaoshan.

You may undertake a spectacular cruise down the Jialing River to the Yangtze River. The 19-mile journey can be made in two hours. The cruise is highly recommended, especially for those visitors who are unable to undertake a journey down the Yangtze to Wuhan or Shanghai. There are regular day and evening cruises.

THREE GORGES

Sailing downstream on the Yangtze from Chongqing to Wuhan, you are surely able to see the world-famous Three Gorges.

In Chongqing, you can take either one of the modern cruisers organized by CITS or one of the older vessels carrying local passengers. The journey downstream to Wuhan takes three days and two nights, and to Shanghai, five days.

The World Famous Three Gorges

On the second day, you come to the three major gorges. Great limestone cliffs tower over either side of Yangtze. The river often narrows to less than 328 ft., and volume of water gushes through.

After passing the three gorges, you travel along miles of rapidly-flowing river until you reach the sanctuary of the central Chinese plain.

GUIYANG

Guiyang is the capital of Guizhou province, located at an elevation of 3,000 feet in the very center of the province. It is dominated by mist-shrouded hills surrounding the Wujiang Valley. The climate is mild throughout the year,

The beautiful scene of the Underground Park

Huang Guo Shu Falls, one of the biggest water falls in China

like that in Kunming, the capital of neighboring Yunnan province.

The original settlement was established under the Han about 2,000 years ago.

The most interesting scenic spot in this city is the Southern Cave, or Underground Park as it is called by the locals. About half a mile in length, the cave contains spectacular stalactites and stalagmites.

A three-hour journey west from Guiyang is the Huang Guo Shu waterfall, one of the biggest falls in China. It is 216 feet high and 246 feet wide. Water pours down a cliff into the Xiniu Pool. Sunlight is diffracted through the drops of water, producing glorious rainbows. There is a natural cave behind the waterfall, 121 feet above Xiniu Pool. Standing inside and watching the water pouring down is an unforgettable sight. Around the Huang Guo Shu are 18 smaller falls and 30 karst caves.

KUNMING

Kunming, the capital of Yunnan province, is known as the "city of eternal spring." Located in the middle of the Yunnan plateau 6,200 feet above sea level, subtropical Kunming is skirted by mountains to the north, east, and west, while to the south lies a large lake called Dianchi. Kunming has a temperate climate and flowers bloom most of the year round, but its association with eternal spring can be misleading, because there are sometimes cold winds in winter, chilly days in spring, and heavy rains in summer. Generally speaking, though, the city's climate is kind to travellers most of the time.

Kunming has a history spanning more than 2,000 years. It is known to have been a small settlement as early as 109

B.C., trading in salt, silver, gold, silk and lumber. Through the eighth to the 13th centuries, it was the secondary capital of a small kingdom in the region, before falling to the Mongols in 1274. A small group of Mongols still exists at Tonghai, about 75 miles due south of Kunming.

Yunnan province, so named because of its location to the south of the Yun Mountains, is the home of 23 ethnic groups including the Han.

Xishan, or West Hill, is a 30-minute bus ride from Kunming. It is realy made up of four hills which form a contour resembling a sleeping beauty, whose hair flows down to the water. For this reason Xishan is also called sleeping beauty mountain. A forest stretches for several miles, containing ancient buildings such as the Huating Temple, the Taihua Temple, and the Sanqing Pavilion, nestling almost unseen, among the thick foliage. From Xishan you can get a fantastic view of Lake Dianchi.

Dianchi, known also as Kunming Lake, covers 120 square miles and was formed by a geological fault in the central Yunnan plateau. It has long been famous for its fish.

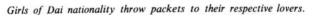
Girls of Dai nationality throw packets to their respective lovers.

Indeed, Marco Polo praised the variety and bounty of catches in his 13th century account of his travels in the region. Now the blue lake is dotted with the many white sails of long, flat boats.

The famous Stone Forest is located 73 miles to the southeast of Kunming within the boundaries of Lunan county. It is also known as the Stone Forest of Lunan.

About 220 million years ago, the area where the Stone Forest now stands was submerged beneath the sea, and deposits of limestone built up there. As a result of countless earthquakes and movements in the Earth's crust, the ground was thrust up and the sea subsided to give way to a tableland. The constant seeping of rain water containing carbonic acid through the cracks in the limestone, gradually dissolved much of the stone and broadened the fissures. Eventually, only great stone pillars remained — a most enchanting formation, which, from a distance, resembles a forest of

pines.

Scattered through this strange landscape are natural and artificial ponds, tiny bridges and classical pavilions. The tallest stone pillar towers 99 feet. The most interesting sights are the "Sword Peak Pond", "Lotus Blossom Peak", "Jade Lake in the Stone Forest", and the "Peak View Pavilion".

You may be interested to catch a glimpse of the interesting costumes and customs of the many ethnic groups in Yunnan.

The best chance is probably at the Water Splashing Festival, a traditional gala held every April to celebrate the new year on the calendar of the Dai, Blang, Benglong, Achang and Wa people. At the festival, people splash water on each other as a symbol of best wishes for a long life and a good harvest. The biggest celebration is usually held in Xishuangbanna, a fertile tropical area about 400 miles south of Kunming.

Singing and dancing, young people of Dai nationality splash water on each other as symbol of best wishes.

The Famous Potala Palace

LHASA

If China's Tibet Autonomous Region is the "roof of the world," then its capital, Lhasa, is certainly the "city of the sun." Standing on a plain over 12,000 feet above sea level, surrounded by towering mountains, Lhasa is a town bathed in sunlight.

Tibet has suffered fluctuating fortunes over the centuries. Historical records reveal little about the region before the seventh century, when King Songzan Ganbu (617-650 A.D.) unified the area and introduced the Sanskrit alphabet. During the centuries that followed, Buddhism took root in Tibet, introduced from India into China by pilgrims travelling the "Silk Road" far to the north.

132

Buddhism was influenced by the local religion, called Bon, and developed into a form called Lamaism. By the 10th century, the religious movement began to assert political leadership as well. In 1572, a reincarnation of Zongkaba, the founder of the "yellow hat" sect devoted to religious reform, became the first Dalai Lama.

POTALA PALACE

The famous Potala Palace was built on the Red Hill of Lhasa in the seventh century. The Tibetan King, Songzan Ganbu, built it for his wife, Princess Wen Cheng of the Tang Dynasty, who had journeyed from Xi'an to Lhasa to marry him. The Potala Palace, a 13-storey building contaning 1,000 rooms, can be seen from many miles away.

THE JOKHANG TEMPLE

The magnificent Jokhang Temple, founded more than 1,300 years ago, is situated in the center of Lhasa. In front of the gate stands a stone tablet from the Tang Dynasty, bearing both Chinese characters and Tibetan script. Nearby is the Tang willow tree planted by Princess Wen Cheng.

DREPUNG MONASTERY

Another famous building in Lhasa is the Drepung Monastery located six miles north of the city. Standing on a high cliff, its many tiers leaning into a steep mountain face, the monastery is built in traditional Tibetan style. Founded in 1416, it was one of the centers of the "yellow hat" sect, and became in its time the largest of the three great monasteries near Lhasa, housing 10,000 lamas. The temples of the monastery are lavishly decorated with statues of the Buddha, Zongkaba, and others of the Buddhist pantheon. The monastery is still open to worshippers.

Peak of the World Famous Mount Qomolangma

MOUNT QOMOLANGMA

Mount Qomolangma, meaning "goddess the third" in the Tibetan language, or Everest as it is known in the West, is the world's highest peak, more than 29,000 feet high.

It is everybody's wish to see the world's highest peak, of course, but it is best to admire it from afar, and leave the climbing to the mountaineers.

134

GUILIN

Guilin, a city named after its lovely osmanthus, is hailed by many as being the most beautiful place in China. In an old Chinese saying, "Guilin overshadows all other cities of China for scenery". Its shapely-rising limestone towers and crystal-clear waters are portrayed in many Chinese works of art. It also has some fascinating caves. The city, which has inspired painters and poets for centuries, is in the northeast corner of the Guangxi Zhuang Autonomous Region.

Guilin was founded in the Qin Dynasty in 214 B.C. as a small settlement on the Lijiang River. It grew following the construction of a canal joining the river with another further north, providing a transport link with the Yangtze. The imperial court could thus send food and provisions by water from the Yangtze plains to its armies in the far south. The town became the provincial capital under the Ming Dynasty, and remained so until 1914, when the capital was moved to Nanning.

Since the founding of the People's Republic in 1949, Guilin has developed a fledging industry, producing pharmaceutical goods, tyres, machinery, fertilizers, silk, and many other items. From its noted profusion of flowering cassia trees, which have a strong, sweet scent, it produces a number of specialities including perfume, wine, tea, cinnamon, and herbal medicine.

There are more than 30 noted scenic spots within the boundaries of Guilin. Among them the most well-known in the city are Duxiu Peak, a hill standing in solitary loftiness in the center of the city; Elephant Trunk Hill, the city's symbol, so named because of its resemblance to an elephant sipping water from the Lijiang River with its trunk; Piled Festoon

Hill that is broken here and there with its rock strata exposed on its sides like piles of fancy festoons; and Crescent Hill that is named after its moon-shaped cave opening.

There are two fantastic caves in the area — the seven-star-rock cave, which derives its name from the arrangement of surrounding peaks resembling the pattern of the stars of the Great Bear constellation, and Reed-Flute Cave, named after the reeds growing around the cave mouth. They both contain spectacular stalactites and stalagmites.

The city also boasts other beautiful hills, such as the Fubo Hill, which is supposed to restrain the waters of the Lijiang River, and Nanxi Hill, that stands magnificently like a huge screen.

A boat trip from Guilin along the Lijiang River will present one of the finest excursions on your tour of China. The journey downstream to Yangshuo offers 30 miles of breathtaking scenery.

Scene of Guilin which claims to have the "finest mountains and rivers under heaven".

Lijiang River in the Sunset

One of the first points of interest is the pagoda-capped Elephant Trunk Hill, or Xiangbishan, long used as the symbol of Guilin. A little further downstream you will pass, on your left, Baotashan with a Ming Dynasty pagoda on top. East of it stands Chuanshan, or the Hill with the Hole. Then begins a series of beautiful scenes that unfold as you glide away from Guilin on your journey south.

On nearing the Erlang Gorge, a huge cliff comes into view. This is the famous "Picture Hill" which resembles horses of different colors in different positions.

On the right, after passing Picture Hill, is Huangbu (Yellow Cloth) Beach. Here the river is wide and flows gently. Seven graceful peaks are likened to seven quiet young girls standing shoulder to shoulder. The fabled Xingping Wonderland begins here. Xingping is a famous, ancient town. Caishi Hill looms high in front of the town, while behind are the five peaks of the majestic Wuzhi Mountains. The area is thick with bamboo groves. As the boat sails near, and disturbs the peace, egrets take wing, adding charm to the picturesque scene.

The cruise ends at the colorful market town of Yangshuo. Your car or bus will then take you back to Guilin. On the way, you will see something of the lush countryside of the province.

SPECIAL ECONOMIC ZONES AND OPEN CITIES

Shenzhen (Shumchun), Zhuhai and Shantou (Swatow) in Guangdong province and Xiamen (Amoy) in Fujian province were designated as Special Economic Zones in 1980 to attract foreign investment in the implementation of the policy of opening China to the outside world. And 14 coastal cities — Beihai, Dalian, Fuzhou, Guangzhou, Lianyungang, Nantong, Ningbo, Qingdao, Qinhuangdao, Shanghai, Tianjin, Wenzhou, Yantai and Zhanjiang — and Hainan Island were opened up to overseas investment and trade in 1984 to develop the open policy further. These zones and cities stretch from north to south along China's Pacific coast. Each with its own special features and advantages in environment and natural conditions, they have become both business centers and tourist attractions.

BEIHAI

Beihai (including the Fangcheng Harbor area) in southern Guangxi Zhuang Autonomous Region is the only coastal city opened to the outside world in China's five autonomous regions inhabited by ethnic minorities. It is a small port city covering an area of 170 miles and with a population of 173,740. Narrow in the south and north, it resembles a rhinoceros horn extending to the sea. The port has an annual handling capacity of 3,600,000 tons. It was from here that the first merchant fleet of the Han Dynasty (206 B.C.-220 A.D.) conducted trade with Malaysia, Indonesia and Burma more than 2,000 years ago. Beihai is one of the world's four biggest fishing ports, and also has an important sea cucumber breeding industry. Prawns, shark's fin, sea horse and groupers abound in local markets, and the area under pearl cultivation covers 33 acres. On display in the aquarium in the Seaside Park are more than 650 species of fish and other sea creatures.

Beihai's genial climate and extensive beaches favor the development of tourism. From the Crest Peak, tourists get a panoramic view of the city and the sea. On the western suburbs, the Lianyang Cave — with stalactites and stalagmites of the most striking colors — resembles the caves at Guilin in the same autonomous region.

DALIAN

Dalian is China's northeast gateway for trade, with a mild marine climate and distinct seasonal changes. Its port — spacious, deep and ice-free—is the country's second-largest harbor after Shanghai. The city has well-developed land, sea and air communications with the outside world.

Because of its mild climate conditions, Dalian is known as China's "home of apples", growing some 50 varieties. It is a major fishing port, and nearly 100 species of fish are shipped in, along with a dozen species of shellfish and many other kinds of seafood thriving in the coastal waters.

Dalian is a well-known summer resort for tourists with its charming scenery and congenial climate. It is endowed with numerous beaches along its long and winding coastline. Sun-bathing is very popular, In the seaside Xinghai (star-sea) Park of 37 acres on a small hill is Tanhai (sea-exploring) Cave, in which stone steps lead down to the sea. Near the cave is a reef, called Xingshi (star stone). According to a legend, a blackfish once fought against a shark that terrorised the area. A star helped the blackfish by throwing a huge rock at the shark, pinning it to the sea bed. The rock now stands on the reef. Standing on the Seaview Tower, tourists can enjoy a good view of the area.

Laohutan (Tiger Beach) Park, southeast of Dalian

Xinghai (Star sea) Park

covers an area of 24.7 acres. It contains the exquisite and elegant Double-Eave Pavilion. On a bluff to the west of the pavilion is a stone stele engraved with the name of the park. Beneath it is Laohu (tiger) Cave.

Legend has it that a ferocious tiger once roamed the beach, attacking local people. A youth called Shi Cao volunteered to get rid of the tiger. He and the tiger died in battle, and Shi was declared a hero. People visiting the park today can see the nearby Half-gone Hill (resembling prostrate tiger with half its head chopped off), the Shicao Hill (resembling a giant lying on the sea and the Tiger's Tooth Reef).

The seawater in the park is crystal clear. Tourists can try their luck by diving into the limpid waters to catch shellfish or enjoy a boat cruise to admire Dalian's coastal landscape.

White Pagoda

FUZHOU

This capital of Fujian province on the southeast China coast, faces Taiwan across the straits. There is neither scorching heat in summer nor severe cold in winter. Trees remain green and flowers bloom the year round.

More than 900 years ago, the prefect of Fuzhou, who loved banyan trees, ordered the local people to grow them everywhere, so the place became known as a city of banyan trees. It is also known as a city of "Sanshan" (three Mountains) after the three surrounding peaks, Yu, Wushi and Ping.

Fuzhou was a town back in the sixth century A.D. Over the years it became a great trading port, selling sugar, wood, tea, fish and tropical fruits overseas, while buying precious stones and pearls from Indian and Arab trading vessels. Marco Polo mentioned the town in his account of his journeys in China.

142

Many scenic spots and historical sites are to be found in this provincial capital. The Drum Hill on the northern bank of Minjiang River, east of the city, is approximately 3,250 ft. high, and gets its name from a huge, flat drum-like rock on top of it. The Yongquan Temple on the hill was built in 908. Kept there are the white jade Sleeping Buddha and the scriptures of various dynasties, all of which are of great value.

At Lingyuan Cave and Drinking Water Rock, to the east of the temple in beautiful and tranquil surroundings, runs clear spring water. On the rocks there are several hundred carvings, rarely seen in southeast China.

West of the temple are 18 caves in a pine forest. From Drum Hill one can get a magnificent view of Fuzhou with the Minjiang River flowing east.

HAINAN ISLAND

Hainan Island in the South China Sea, at about the

Coconut-palm forest

same latitude with Hawaii, is China's second-largest island after Taiwan. It covers 2,125 sq. miles, and is inhabited by 5,600,000 people of Han, Li, Miao, Hui and other ethnic groups. It has been referred to as a "treasure island". An abundance of tropical crops such as coconuts, rubber and lemongrass are grown, and the island is rich in aquatic products and mineral resources.

The Shilu Mine, in western Hainan, is China's largest open-cast iron mine. Its ore has a 70 percent iron content. The Yinggehai and the Beibu Gulf oilfields, the largest in the South China Sea, are both located near Hainan.

A vast primeval forest there contains specimens of 40 percent of the country's rare plant species under state protection.

For historical reasons, Hainan Island remained out of touch with the rest of the world for centuries. It used to be considered remote and primitive enough to be a suitable place of exile for disgraced officials and poets, and this image — isolation, scorching sun, humid weather and dense virgin forest infested with various snakes and beasts of prey — did not change until the ninth century A.D.

Now, Hainan Island has excellent sea and air links with the outside world. It is only 30 minutes by air from Guangzhou. The vast tropical rain forest of 822,677 acres on the island offers a variety of treasures. Some precious trees there are made of wood so hard that a three-horsepower chainsaw has difficulty cutting into it.

A rich variety of wildlife lives in the jungle. Hainan is the home of more than 80 species of animal and 340 varieties of bird. The rarest animal is the Hainan deer which is protected by the state. On the Nanwan Peninsula in southern Hainan, 600 rhesus monkeys live in 16 groups in an official rhesus monkey reserve.

Tourists can enjoy the natural beauty of Hainan island. From the Haikou Tourist Resort one can seek out the ancient temples built in memory of some of the exiled dignitaries. Interesting trips can be made into the tropical rain forest and to Rhesus Monkey Hill. Hainan is warm all year round, and makes an ideal winter holiday resort.

LIANYUNGANG

Lianyungang is a port city in Jiangsu province.

Known as Haizhou in ancient times, it has a history of about 2,000 years. It first became a trading port in the Han Dynasty and by the ninth century A.D. 10 oceangoing ships could anchor simultaneously at the port.

Lianyungang is a richly-endowed city in terms of scenery — hills, plains and beaches — and various mineral resources. It covers about 3,750 sq. miles. It's climate is warm and moist, and many varieties of animals, plants, fish and other aquatic creatures live in the area. There has been considerable development in recent years of agriculture, forestry, animal husbandry, side-line production, fishing and salt and mineral production.

With 14 scenic districts and over 100 scenic spots, the city features "greatness, ancientry, mystery and quietness". It has been a good place for holiday makers and a well-known summer resort. Yuntai Mountain, 15 miles to the city, is famed for its scenery. The lofty mountain, enclosed by cloud and mist, is well-known for its Huaguoshan (Flower and Fruit Hill) and Shuiliandong (Water Cave) which were described in the renowned Chinese fairy tale "The Pilgrimage to the West." People associate the famous Monkey King, a character in the legend, with the hill. The Town Sucheng is another scenic spot of Yuntai Mountain. With mountains behind and sea in front, it is a very beautiful place which has long been called "The Land of Peach Blossoms."

NANTONG

Nantong, on the north bank of the Yangtze River estuary, was first built in 958.

The city and surrounding districts covers an area of 5,000 sq. miles, and has a population of 400,000.

Nantong's textiles and light industries have enjoyed a long and successful history. The mild climate and fertile soil enable the area to grow many profitable crops, such as cotton, peppermint and spearmint. Nantong's clams and jellyfish are sold to many countries.

The area has many beauty spots and is criss-crossed with lovely waterways. A poet once described Nantong as "a piece of jade on the Yangtze".

The Haohe River winds past busy streets and quiet back lanes, lined on both banks with weeping willows.

In the southern suburbs, Mount Wolf towers over the Yangtze.

It is regarded as one of China's eight small Buddhist mountains. In a gallery on its slopes are stone tablets inscribed by 18 ancient monks — one of them Japanese — along with vivid portraits of them.

At the foot of the hill, Lo Bingwang's tomb is shaded among shrubs. A scholar in the Tang Dynasty, Lo wrote a Call to Arms against Empress Wu Zetian — a masterpiece still marvelled by classical Chinese historians.

Also in the southern suburbs is the Zhang Qian Tomb, which is actually a serene park. Zhang Qian was the last Supreme Scholar of the Qing Dynasty.

Descending the northern slope of Mount Wolf, one approaches the Northern Foot Garden. It commands a magnificent view, while nearby are many caves and crags, on which inscriptions have been carved by noted Chinese calligraphers, such as Wu Changshuo in the late Qing Dynasty.

Dawning of Ningbo

NINGBO

This city lives up to its reputation as "a jewel by the sea". Some 220 miles south of Shanghai, it is an ancient port city. It began to trade with neighboring countries more than 1,200 ago. After the Opium War (1840-42), Ningbo was forced to open to the West as a treaty port.

Modern Ningbo comprises four districts and seven counties covering an area of 5,873 sq. miles with a population of 4,810,000. Situated half way along the coastline between the big northern ports of Dalian and Tianjin in the north and Guangzhou and Hongkong in the south, Ningbo is well placed geographically for trade. Its harbor at the mouth of the Yongjiang River is 20 meters deep. It includes enough space for the construction of dozens of deep-water berths to accommodate 100,000-ton ships.

The navigation channels to the East China Sea can accommodate 150,000-class freighters, and even 200,000 tonners may call at the harbor at high tide.

Ningbo is also the second-largest industrial city in Zhejiang province, with more than 5,000 factories employing 556,000 workers.

Ningbo is blessed with many historical sites and scenic spots.

Putuo Mountain, one of the five famous Buddhist shrines of China, is on a small island facing Ningbo. Many worshippers stop at Ningbo before or after making a pilgrimage to Putuo, which gives the city a slight religious atmosphere.

The 1,700-year-old Ayuwang Temple is famous because it contains the relics of Sakyamuni Buddha. Looking splendid in green and gold, the temple is surrounded by tall verdant pines and camphor trees. Stele, stone carvings and Buddhist scriptures in the temple are well preserved.

Tianyige Library, established in 1561, is one of the oldest libraries in China. Among its books are the most valuable Ming Dynasty local histories and lists of successful candidates of the imperial examinations. Its shelves have now been greatly enlarged to include many books, transcripts and manuscripts from the Song to the Qing dynasties (960-1911 A.D.).

QINGDAO

The thick, leafy trees, which cover mountains sloping gently to the sea around this city on the southern side of the Shandong Peninsula, have given it the name — Qingdao or "Green Isle". Qingdao covers an area of 3,688 square miles and has a population of 4,100,000 million.

Laoshan Mineral Spring, whose water is used for brewing the famed Qingdao Beer.

You can see the Pacific Ocean from almost everywhere in Qingdao. Its inhabitants live with the constant rhythm of the waves pounding the shore, and inhale the fresh, salty air. It is the sea that has given it great potential for prosperity. In Qingdao's Museum of Aquatic Products, the largest aquarium in China, 60 tanks display the wealth of the sea.

Qingdao possesses six bathing beaches. Their smooth sands slope gently to the sea. With beautiful natural landscape, Badaguan (Eight Passes Area) is a well-known sanatorium quarter.

Laoshan Mountains, which soar up to 3,626 ft. above the sea, stand majestically, commanding a magnificent view east of the city. Laoshan spring water, crystal clear and pleasant to taste, is the source for the famed Qingdao Beer and Laoshan mineral water.

149

Fourty-seven miles northeast of Qingdao city is Jimo hot spring. The highest temperature of the spring is 90 degrees Centigrade, although is generally kept at between 37 and 38 degrees. The spring water contains many minerals which can bring relief from rheumatic and arthritic complaints and psoriasis.

Visitors can enjoy a panoramic view of the Qingdao coastline from the Pier built in 1891, in the center of Qingdao Bay.

A stroll in the old part of the city will reveal a good variety of villas, cathedrals and houses in German, Spanish and Japanese style, all built during the period when Qingdao was occupied successively by Germany and Japan from 1897 to 1945.

QINHUANGDAO

Qinhuangdao, or "Qin Emperor's Island", is so named because it is said that soldiers sent by the first emperor of the Qin Dynasty to search for immortality medicines rested and passed through this region.

Facing the Pacific Ocean and screened by mountains, it is an important ice-free port in northern China's Hebei province. The city consists of three districts — Shanhaiguan, Beidaihe and Haigang — with a total population of 320,000.

Shanhaiguan, also called "the First Pass under Heaven", is the starting point of the Great Wall. It has been a strategic point since ancient times. The eye can feast on mile upon mile of silvery waves crashing onto steep cliffs. From the gate tower, you can see the Great Wall, like a dragon winding its way along the mountain ridges, and disappearing beyond the horizon. Inside the gate tower, you can rent an ancient costume, and, holding an ancient weapon, have your pictures taken.

Beidaihe is a seaside resort set on the bay of Bohai. It

Beidaihe bathing beach

enjoys an intoxicating mixture of warm sunshine and cool sea breezes from mid-May to October.

Reminiscent of a Mediterranean holiday town but without the high-rise hotels, Beidaihe is a cluster of villas, mostly built for European businessmen in the early part of the century, strung out along six miles of sandy beaches. The attractive village is complete with seafood restaurants and ice-cream parlors.

SHANTOU

Shantou (Swatow) is situated in eastern Guangdong province, adjacent to Hongkong and Macao, and facing the South China Sea. It occupies an area of 6,613 square miles and has a population of nearly 720,000. Shantou has been a long-standing trading port, with a reputation for high quality light industrial products such as drawn-works and photographic paper.

Since its establishment as a Special Economic Zone, this agricultural area is burgeoning as a major processing center for exports, and is attracting considerable foreign and overseas Chinese investment.

The one mile Longhu village, in the eastern suburbs of Shantou, is mainly devoted to the processing industry. East of Shantou Harbor, new docks are being built to handle the growing trade.

New tourist facilities have sprung up in and around Shantou. Among the best places to visit are Mayu Island, Qingyun Crag and the Lotus Flower Cliff in Haimen county.

Holiday makers can feast on the tropical fruits grown there, which include litchis, pineapples, bananas and oranges.

SHENZHEN

Bordering on Hongkong, in southern China's Guangdong province, Shenzhen covers 204 sq. miles and has a population of 300,000. Close to the Shenzhen Railway Station is the New Luohu District, the financial and commercial center, with many high-rise buildings. Farther out lie Shangbu and Bagualing, two industrial districts containing many electronics, textiles, food and other light industrial plants.

The tropical location, natural charm and modern facilities have turned Shenzhen into a popular and well-equipped tourist resort, with many villas, hotels, scenic spots and entertainment facilities.

Nineteen miles southwest of the city proper, facing Shenzhen Bay, is Shekou area with blue water, yellow sandy beaches and green gardens lined with palm trees. Big attractions there include the "Sea World" entertainment center, an exhibition of ancient terracotta warriors and Qing Dynasty houses.

The Silver Lake resort, shaded by pines on a hillside on the northern edge of Shenzhen, combines fine architectural design and elegant interior decor. Villas there are replicas of historic mansions, each providing an excellent blend of privacy and comfort.

Shenzhen itself has a long white sandy beach and many winding waterways, spreading out against a background of towering hills. Flowing eastward into Dapeng Bay in the South China Sea, three rivers divide the flat beach into four sections — all being excellent bathing areas. Away from the shore are the inland scenic spots of Xili (West Beauty) resort and the new reservoir.

Developing Shenzhen City

TIANJIN

Tianjin, meaning "Port to Heavenly Capital', is 87 miles southeast of Beijing, on the coast of the Bohai Sea. China's third-largest city with a population of 7,790,000, it is one of the three municipalities directly under the central government.

Its location at the confluence of five tributaries of the Haihe River, as well as at the junction of the Beijing-Shanhaiguan and Tianjin-Pukou railways, makes it a hub of convenient land and water transportation.

First settled in the Song Dynasty (960-1279 A.D.), Tianjin became important in the 14th century, when grain, carried to Beijing along the Grand Canal that linked the North with the South, was stored there. By the 15th century it had become a garrison town enclosed by walls.

The French Cathedral in Tianjin

However, it suffered during the Yihetuan Uprising (or "Boxer Revolution") in 1900, when the rebels dug in behind the walls of the old town. After Tianjin was captured, the European invaders tore down the walls to make sure that Tianjin could never again be used as a sanctuary.

During those chaotic years, Tianjin was one of the first Chinese cities to set up a fledging modern industry. After several decades of development, Tianjin is now one of China's leading manufacturing and commercial centers.

The past millennium has left Tianjin with many historical sites, such as Mount Pan in the suburban Jixian county, the 1,000-year-old Dule Temple (Temple of Solitary Joy), an elegant mosque, a huge cathedral, the picturesque Shuishang Park (Water Park) and the Ningyuan Garden (Garden of Tranquillity), which is studded with many traditional Chinese-style structures threaded together by a long corridor.

WATER PARK

Located in the southwest of Tianjin, the park is built on three lakes with 13 inlets scattered over 247 ac. of water. Pavilions, towers and terraces dot the banks, and facilities are provided for swimming and sailing. The Shuishang Dengyinglou Restaurant overlooking the lakes serves marvellous freshwater fish and prawns.

GARDEN OF TRANQUILLITY

The park is in the style of a traditional Chinese garden, and is believed to have been built by Yuan Shikai, a notorious military general of the late Qing Dynasty. Covering an area of 133 ac., one third of it water, the park is studded with Qing-style pavilions, arches and corridors. Among the many trees and flowers is a theater and a restaurant serving Mongolian barbecues.

JIXIAN COUNTY

Situated on the Tianjin outskirts, 78 miles north of the city proper, Jixian county contains many places of interest. Among them are the ancient Dule Temple (Temple of Solitary Joy), the Longquan Garden where a 1,000-year-old "scholar" tree grows, the Impregnable Pass where part of the Great Wall passes, and the enchanting Mount Pan.

The Dule Temple is located in Jixian county town. First built in the Tang Dynasty, it is famous for its superb wooden structure, its 16-meter-high sculpture of the Goddess Guanyin and its colorful frescoes. Legend has it that when An Lushan, a Tang Dynasty general, rebelled against the emperor, he held a rally at the temple before going to war, and gave the temple its name "Solitary Joy" because he wanted happiness exclusively for himself.

To the northwest of the county seat lies Mount Pan, a favorite mountain resort for many emperors over the centuries. The path up is flanked by numerous scenic spots, each with an interesting legend behind it.

There is a beautiful pine forest on top of the mountain, fantastic rock formations about half way up.

WENZHOU

Wenzhou, 320 nautical miles south of Shanghai and 660 nautical miles north of Hongkong, is an important city in eastern Zhejiang province with a population of 500,000. Wenzhou, or "Mild Land", has a mild climate averaging 18 degrees centigrade all the year round.

As an ancient port, it traded with southeast Asian countries as early as the 11th-12th century. It faces the East China Sea, with hills on three sides, and is renowned for its charming scenery and its sweet, juicy citrus fruit, which is sold abroad.

The Mid-River Isle in the city looks like a ship with two

pagodas at either end acting as two masts. The "Lovers' Tree" greets the eyes of visitors to the isle. The 800-year-old tree is actually a camphor tree intertwined with a banyan.

Strolling on through a round door, the visitor enters a garden of willows, a pavilion and a lake spanned by a bridge. In winter from this spot, one can see the glitering Mount Luofu on the north bank of the river looking as if snow is drifting in the air. A horizontal board hungs on the small pavilion bearing the inscription "Snow-Coming Pavilion" written by the late Chinese scholar, Guo Moruo.

Other places of interest in Wenzhou include the nearby Mount Yandang and the Chengtian Hot Spring, which contains radon, said to be good for relieving high blood pressure, rheumatic arthritis, Cardiovascular diseases and skin ailments. Yandang is known for its overhanging cliffs, strangely-shaped rocks, clear rivers and beautiful trees and flowers.

Village takes on a new look in Wenzhou

XIAMEN (AMOY)

Xiamen, known in the native Fujian dialect as Amoy, is an island off the coast of southeast China. The shape of the island is said to resemble a flying egret. Centuries ago it was, in fact, an uninhabited island nesting site for these birds. Folk tales recount battles between the egrets and poisonous snakes for dominance over the island.Now, Xiamen is also known as the Island of the Egret.

The island's history can be traced back 3,000 years. Ming Emperor Zhu Hongwu (1328-1398 A.D.) ordered a new city to be built there to guard against pirates. He named it Xiamen, meaning the Gate to the Chinese Mansion. National hero Zheng Chenggong (1624-1662 A.D.) once headed a garrison there. After the Opium War in 1840, it became one of the five ports forced open to trade by foreign powers.

With an area of 324 square miles and a population of 960,000, it is now the second-largest city in Fujian province. Surrounded by rocks, caves, temples, gardens, flowers and woods, it has a variety of natural and cultural scenic spots.

To the southwest lies Gulangyu Isle. It is a land of flowers, swaying palms and tropical fruit. On top of the Rock of Sunshine there, is a 23 ft. platform supporting a memorial hall to Zheng Chenggong. One can descend from the hill to Shuzhuang Garden and then down a winding path to a soft sandy beach below.

Longtou (Dragon's Head) Hill rises to face Hutou (Tiger's Head) Hill across the channel at Xiamen. From the top of Longtou, the islet appears to be a sea of green trees and redtiled roofs. Houses and streets cling in tiers to the side of the hill. Below is a cool cave containing strange rock formations, called "Summer Resort" Cave.

For tourists to get a better view of the sea and beaches,

Xiamen recently launched the "Lujiang" (touring the sea), a floating hotel with 700 beds, restaurant and recreation facilities.

YANTAI

Yantai, or "Smoke Tower", is a port city in Shandong province. The name dates back to the 14th century, when the area was a strategic defence outpost. When the occupants wanted to give the alarm, they burnt wolf dung. Smoke from a tower could be seen for miles.

Yantai remained a small fishing village until the 19th century when it opened to foreign trade.

Now, the city covers 140 square miles and has a population of 385,000. Yantai harbor is wide and deep, and ice-free all year round.

In southern Yantai is a chain of undulating hills, and in the north are several attractive islands, such as Zhifu and Kongtong. Yuhuang Peak, with an ancient edifice commanding an excellent view of the city, is a scenic spot of haunting beauty.

Some 44 miles away from Yantai city is Penglai Pavilion on Danya Hill. The pavilion, named after the Fabled Abode of Immortals, reaches up towards the sky majestically, and commands a great view of the sea. It has a fairyland atmosphere, and since ancient times, it has regularly attracted poets and scholars, who have come to enjoy the scenery or to sing its praises. Penglai Pavilion is famed for its mirages. On fine days in early summer, an infinite variety of fantastic and miraculous scenes sometimes appear above the quiet surface of the sea.

Tropical seaside scene

ZHANJIANG

Zhanjiang is a fledging port city in the northeast of the Leizhou Peninsula in Guangdong province, it is the closest Chinese port to Southeast Asia, Oceania, Africa and Europe. It has air, rail and bus links with Guangzhou, Shenzhen and Hongkong. Tourists can also travel to and from Hongkong by sea.

Zhanjiang has conditions favorable for beach farming, particularly pear breeding.

Zhanjiang is also a tourist spot, with tropical seaside scenery, striking ancient landforms and many examples of classical culture.

Donghai Island, 12.5 miles offshore from Zhanjiang city, is the most interesting tourist spot among the isles scattered along Zhanjiang's 813 mile-long coastline. It covers 200 square miles to rank fifth in size among China's 5,000 islands. From the island, the view is one of seabirds flying amid white clouds above canvas-roofed fishing boats undulating on the silver tide. Donghai Island is cool because of its dense forest. To the south of the forest, a 10-mile beach forms a gleaming crescent. Forest, beach, sunshine and sea unite to form an area resembling the Spanish "sunshine coast". There is superb seafood cuisine. A fishing ground surrounds the island, teaming with abalone, lobster, prawn, crab and shellfish.

The Leizhou Peninsula at Zhanjiang contains 56 ancient craters, proving that the area was volcanic 600,000 to 1,000,000 years ago. Among these craters is the well-preserved lake luster crag.

There is the world's largest man-made forest covering 590,000 ac. There are 77 varieties of eucalyptus, some of them rare species.

Zhanjiang has many cultural relics and historical sites; it was inhabited by ethnic groups before the Song Dynasty, and used as a place of exile for dissidents in feudal times.

ZHUHAI

The city of Zhuhai is situated on the west bank of the Pearl River estuary adjacent to Macao, 70 minutes from Hongkong by hydrofoil. It has an area of 116 sq. mi and a population of 150,000. In October, 1980, a 10 sq. mi. area there was designated a Special Economic Zone. Since then, eight new highways and a number of electronics, textile, clothing, machinery and furniture factories have been built in the former fishing village.

Now dotting the surrounding hillsides and beaches are new tourist facilities and hotels. Among the bestknown is the Shijingshan Tourist Center—a hexagonal Spanish-style building with 180 rooms. The complex is arranged in the shape of a Chinese character, formed by a group of three squares.

161

The Zhuhai Resort comprises countyards, pavilions, streams, ponds and rocks, and has been built in typical southern Guangdong style. The resort is spread gracefully at the foot of Diting Mountain. Carved on a nearby cliff are figures of the characters, Pigsy, Sandy, Monkey and Tripitaka, from the renowned Chinese novel, "Pilgrimage to the West".

Gongbei Palace Hotel with its 310 rooms is modelled on the Qin Dynasty (221-207 B. C.). In addition to the main hotel guestrooms are 53 villas facing the South China Sea, offering a marvellous view, especially at sunrise or sunset.

Scene of Zhuhai City

SPEAKING THE LANGUAGE

The Chinese written language consists of some 50,000 characters, or ideograms, of which around 10,000 are still in modern usage.

However, pronunciation of these ideograms varies enormously from region to region, since there are many dialects such as Cantonese in Guangdong province, Fujianese in Fujian province and Shanghainese in Shanghai.

A long-term plan has been drawn up to reform the written Chinese language, with the ultimate goal of developing a written language based on a phonetic alphabet. This is a difficult task, and it is likely to take generations to achieve.

Therefore, there is a standard spoken language based on the predominant dialect of north China with Beijing pronunciation, which is known as Mandarin, or Putonghua (common speech).

One major difficulty for foreigners is the existence of two forms of romanisation—Wade-Giles and Pinyin. The latter has recently been adopted officially, and all street names, bus stops and other signs are spelt in this way.

Five letters in particular cause problems for those familiar with the roman alphabet:

"x" is pronounced somewhere between an "s" and "sh"; "sh" sounds like the "sh" in "she"; "q" is as "ch" in "cheek"—not "qu" as in "quick"; "c" sounds like "ts" as in "its"; "i" is either pronounced as "ea" in "eat", or as the "i" in "sir" after the consonants c, ch, r, s, sh, z and zh.

You don't have to worry about the language barrier, though, for in China, apart from the numerous English enthusiasts who are keen to give you friendly help while practicing their English, there are many waiters and shop-assistants in hotels and shops for foreigners who can speak a little English. And there are the omnipresent guides and interpreters provided by your host organizations and travel agencies, although their English may vary from excellence to poor.

But you will find it convenient and sociable to speak a few Chinese words or sentences. The following expressions will never fail you when you want to show your friendliness, or when you are badly in need of something.

Beihai Park in Beijing

DIFFERENCES BETWEEN
CHINESE PHONETIC ALPHABET AND WADE SYSTEM

Pinyin	Wade	Pinyin	Wade
ba	pa	che	ch'ê
bai	pai	chen	ch'ên
ban	pan	cheng	ch'êng
bang	pang	chi	ch'ih
bao	pao	chong	ch'ung
bei	pei	chou	ch'ou
ben	pên	chu	ch'u
beng	pêng	chua	ch'ua
bi	pi	chuai	ch'uai
bian	pien	chuan	ch'uan
biao	piao	chuang	
bie	pieh		ch'uang
bin	pin	chui	ch'ui
bing	ping	chun	ch'un
bo	po	chuo	ch'o
bu	pu	ci	tz'ŭ(ts'ŭ)
ca	ts'a	cong	ts'ung
cai	ts'ai	cou	ts'ou
can	ts'an	cu	ts'u
cang	ts'ang	cuan	ts'uan
cao	ts'ao	cui	ts'ui
ce	ts'ê	cun	ts'un
cen	ts'ên	cuo	ts'o
ceng	ts'êng	da	ta
cha	ch'a	dai	tai
chai	ch'ai	dan	tan
chan	ch'an	dang	tang
chang	ch'ang	dao	tao
chao	ch'ao	de	tê

165

Pinyin	Wade	Pinyin	Wade
deng	têng	guan	kuan
di	ti	guang	kuang
dian	tien	gui	kui
diao	tiao	gun	kun
die	tieh	guo	kuo
ding	ting	he	hê,ho
diu	tiu	hei	hei
dong	tung	hen	hên
dou	tou	heng	hêng
du	tu	hong	hung
duan	tuan	ji	chi
dui	tui	jia	chia
dun	tun	jian	chien
duo	to	jiang	chiang
e	ê	jiao	chiao
ê	eh	jie	chieh
eng	êng	jin	chin
er	êrh	jing	ching
ga	ka	jiong	chiung
gai	kai	jiu	chiu
		ju	chü
gan	kan	juan	chüan
gang	kang	jue	chüeh, chüo
gao	kao	jun	chün
ge	kê,ko	ka	k'a
gei	kei	kai	k'ai
gen	kên	kan	k'an
geng	kêng	kang	k'ang
gong	kung	kao	k'ao
gou	kou	ke	k'ê,k'o
gu	ku	ken	k'ên
gua	kua	keng	k'êng
guai	kuai	kong	k'ung

Pinyin	Wade	Pinyin	Wade
kou	k'ou	pa	p'a
ku	k'u	pai	p'ai
kua	k'ua	pan	p'an
kuai	k'uai	pang	p'ang
kuan	k'uan	pao	p'ao
kuang	k'uang	pei	p'ei
kui	k'ui	pen	p'ên
kun	k'un	peng	p'êng
kuo	k'uo	pi	p'i
le	lê,lo	pian	p'ien
lei	lei	piao	p'iao
leng	lêng	pei	p'ieh
lian	lien	pin	p'in
lie	lieh	ping	p'ing
long	lung	po	p'o
lu	lu	pou	p'ou
		pu	p'u
lue	lüeh,	qi	ch'i
	lüo,	qia	ch'ia
	lio	qian	ch'ien
lun	lun	qiang	ch'iang
mian	mien	qiao	ch'iao
mie	mieh		
nian	nien	qie	ch'ieh
niang	niang	qin	ch'in
niao	niao	qing	ch'ing
nie	nieh	qiong	ch'iung
nu	nü	qiu	ch'iu
nuan	nuan	qu	ch'ü
nüe	nüeh	quan	ch'üan
	nüo	que	ch'üeh
	nio		ch'üo
nuo	no	qun	ch'ün

Pinyin	Wade	Pinyin	Wade
ran	jan	tian	t'ien
rang	jang	tiao	t'iao
rao	jao	tie	t'ieh
re	jê	ting	t'ing
ren	jên	tong	t'ung
reng	jêng	tou	t'ou
ri	jih	tu	t'u
rong	jung	tuan	t'uan
rou	jou	tui	t'ui
ru	ju	tun	t'un
ruan	juan	tuo	t'o
rui	jui	wen	wen
run	jun	weng	weng
ruo	jo	xi	hsi
se	sê	xia	hsia
sen	sên	xian	hsien
seng	sêng	xiang	hsiang
she	shê	xiao	hsiao
shen	shên	xie	hsieh
sheng	shêng	xin	hsin
shi	shih	xing	hsing
si	sŭ, szŭ, ssŭ	xiong	hsiung
		xiu	hsiu
song	sung		
suo	so	xu	hsü
ta	t'a	xuan	hsüan
tai	t'ai	xue	hsüeh, hsüo
tan	t'an	xun	hsün
tang	t'ang	yan	yen
tao	t'ao	ye	yeh
te	t'ê	yong	yung
teng	t'êng	you	yu
ti	t'i	yu	yü

168

Pinyin	Wade	Pinyin	Wade
yuan	yüen	zheng	chêng
yue	yüeh	zhi	chih
yun	yün	zhong	chung
za	tsa	zhou	chou
zai	tsai	zhu	chu
zan	tsan	zhua	chua
zang	tsang	zhuai	chuai
zao	tsao	zhuan	chuan
ze	tsê	zhuang	chuang
zei	tsei	zhui	chui
zen	tsên	zhun	chun
zeng	tsêng	zhuo	cho
zha	cha	zi	tzǔ(tsǔ)
zhai	chai	zong	tsung
zhan	chan	zou	tsou
zhang	chang	zu	tsu
zhao	chao	zuan	tsuan
zhe	chê	zui	tsui
zhei	chei	zun	tsun
zhen	chên	zuo	tso

SHORT CONVERSATIONS

GREETINGS

Ni hao.   "How are you?" or "How do you do?"

Ni Hao is a universal greeting you can use nearly everywhere and at anytime. However, there are some other expressions you may find useful in demonstrating your friendliness or intimacy.

Mang ma?   "Are you busy?" (or "What's up?" —a greeting addressed to people you are familiar with).

Chi fan le ma? "Have you eaten yet?" (used around meal time).

Zen me yang? "How's everything?" or "How are you doing?"

THANKS AND APOLOGIES

Xie xie.   "Thank you." (an expression that cannot be overused).

Fei chang gan "Thank you very much."
xie.

Bu yong xie. "You are welcome."

Bu ke qi.   "Don't mention it."

Dui bu qi.   "I'm sorry." (or "excuse me" when you have done nothing wrong.)

Tai dui bu qi "Im terribly sorry."

Mei guan xi. "It doesn't matter."

Bu yao jin. "It's OK."

USEFUL WORDS

Ganbei!	"Cheers!"
Tai hao le.	"Very good."
Zhong guo.	"China"
Zhong guo tai hao le	"China is wonderful."
Youyi.	"Friendship"
Qing.	"Please."
Jin lai.	"Come in."
Qing zuo.	"Sit down, please."
Gui xing?	"What's your name?"
Zai jian.	"Goodbye."

TELEPHONIN

Qing jie ...	"Extension number ... please."
Wei, shui ya?	"Hello, who is calling?"
Wo shi ...	"It's ... speaking."
Ni Zhao shui?	"Who do you want to speak to?"
Wo zhao ...	"I want ..."
Ta bu zai.	"He/She is not here."
Qing deng yi deng.	"Wait a moment, please."

ASKING THE WAY

Qu ... zen me zou?	"Will you show me the way to ..."
Xiang zuo guai.	"Turn left."
Xiang you guai.	"Turn right."
Yi zhi zou.	"Straight on."

Zuo ji lu gong gong qi che.	"What bus takes me there?"
Na li xia che?	"Where shall I get off the bus?"
Chu zu qi che zhan zai na li?	"Where is a taxi station?"

SHOPPING

Wo yao zhe ge.	"I want this."
Wo yao na ge.	"I want that."
Wo yao da yi dian de.	"I want a bigger one."
Wo yao xiao yi dian de.	"I want a smaller one."
Hai yao yi ge.	"I wnat one more."

Duo shao qian?	"How much is it?"
Yi kuai (yi yuan)	One yuan
Yi mao (yi jiao)	Ten cents
Yi fen	One cent
Shi kuai (shi yuan)	Ten yuan
Yi bai kuai (yi bai yuan)	One hundred yuan

SOS!

Jiu ming!	"Help!" (pronounced as "joe ming". An all-purpose emergency call, literally meaning "save my life". You can use it whenever you are really in danger, but don't abuse it).
Qing jiao jing cha.	"Call the police, please."

The safest way of asking for help when in an emergency, however, is to show the following to anyone nearby with the entry of the help required marked:

I'm a foreign tourist. I'm in trouble. Please:

我是外国旅游者。 现在遇到了麻烦。 请:

* Call an ambulance. I'm injured (or I'm ill).

叫一辆救护车! 我受伤了(我生病了。)

* Take me to a hospital.
  送我上医院。

* Show me the way to ⋯ hotel. I am lost.
  告诉我……旅馆怎么走。 我迷路了。

* Help me dial this number⋯
  帮我拨这个电话……

  119
  火警　fire!

  110
  匪警　robbery!

* Call the police!
  叫警察!

NUMERALS

1	yi	11	shi yi	30	san shi
2	er	12	shi er	40	si shi
3	san	13	shi san	50	wu shi
4	si	14	shi si	60	liu shi
5	wu	15	shi wu	70	qi shi
6	liu	16	shi liu	80	ba shi
7	qi	17	shi qi	90	jiu shi
8	ba	18	shi ba	100	yi bai
9	jiu	19	shi jiu	1,000	yi qian
10	shi	20	er shi	100,000	shi wan

TRANSPORT AND COMMUNICATIONS

TRANSPORT

AIRWAY

The fastest and most convenient way of travelling to and around China is, of course, by air. You can fly from a number of the world's major cities, including Aden, Addis Ababa, Baghdad, Bahrain, Bangkok, Belgrade, Bombay, Bucharest, Delhi, Dubai, Frankfurt, Geneva, Hongkong, Karachi, London, Los Angeles, Manila, Moscow, Nagasaki, New York, Osaka, Paris, Pyongyang, Rangoon, Rawalpindi, Rome, San Francisco, Sharjah, Sydney, Tehran, Tokyo and Zurich.

China's air services have undergone a major decentralization reform. The Civil Aviation Administration of China (CAAC) now operates only as a government department in overall charge of civil aviation affairs. The Beijing-based China Airways (CA) provides international services, and the Shanghai-based China Eastern Airways, the Guangzhou-based China Southern Airways, the Chengdu-based China Southwest Airways and a number of other companies operate domestic services.

All the major Chinese cities are linked by airlines.

RESERVATIONS: Passengers can reserve their seats at CA's booking offices or through its booking agents. But remember to purchase your tickets at the appointed time before noon the day before the flight. Failure to do so means automatic cancellation of the reservation.

RECONFIRMATION OF RESERVATION: If you break your journey for more than 72 hours at any point on the international service of CA you are required to reconfirm your intention of using the continuing or return seat reserved

175

at least 72 hours before the flight departure. Failure to do so will result in the cancellation of the reservation. This provision, however, does not apply to CA flights when all legs of the trip are within Europe.

TICKETS: Domestic tickets are valid for 90 days, and international tickets are valid for one year—both from the date of commencement of travel. If a passenger holding a domestic tecket fails to appear for a scheduled flight, the ticket will be declared void, and no refund will be granted. If a passenger holding an international ticket fails to appear for a scheduled flight, a "no-show" charge will be assessed at 25 percent of the applicable one-way fare for the portions not flown or for the first leg of the journey if it exceeds six hours.

CANCELLATION: If passengers on domestic flights apply for cancellation of a ticket two hours before the scheduled departure time, a cancellation fee of RMB 4.00 (about 1.40 U.S. dollars at time of publication) will be charged or if the value of the ticket is less than RMB 20.00 (about seven U.S. dellars), the cancellation fee will be RMB 1.00 (about 0.35 U.S. dollars). If the request for cancellation is made less than two hours before the scheduled departure time, a fee equal to 20 percent of the ticket fare will be charged. No cancellation fee is charged on infant tickets which were purchased at 10 percent of the full fare. A full refund will be made to passengers holding international tickets if cancellation is made before the airport check-in time.

HEALTH REQUIREMENTS: Passengers suffering from serious illness or contagious diseases must possess a doctor's certificate, and with the agreement of CA officials can then make reservations and obtain tickets.

BAGGAGE: The free baggage allowances are 30 kgs. (66 lbs.) for a first-class passenger, and 20 kgs. (44 lbs.) for an economy-class passenger. Hand baggage is limited to 5 kgs. (11 lbs.)

AIRPORT FEE: Passengers leaving China from any international airport in the country, whether travelling by CA or other airlines, are each required to pay 10 yuan (about 3-5 U.S. dollars) in airport fees. However, holders of diplomatic passports, transit passengers and children under 12 are exempt.

RAILWAYS

If you are a train lover and have plenty of time, you will enjoy travelling to and around China by train. There is the adventurous Trans-Siberian Railway from Moscow to Beijing, which takes six days and costs only 130 U. S. dollars for a deluxe accommodation equipped with shower. There are also the Pyongyang-Beijing and Hongkong-Guangzhou expresses, as well as the many regular train services.

Inside China, the railway network stretches over 31,000 miles, and links all the major cities except Lhasa, capital of Tibet. Long rides pass through different climatic and geographic areas, offering the traveller a feast of varied scenery.

Chinese trains are comfortable and clean. Tea and other refreshments are offered at moderate prices and at regular intervals during your journey. There is a dining car and you can order meals in your own compartment.

There are three kinds of domestic train ticket with two price levels for each:

Regular: soft or hard-seat.
Express fare: regular or special.
Sleeping-coach fare: soft or hard berth.

Your travel guides will handle the tickets.

URBAN TRAFFIC

One of the spectacles in large Chinese cities is the

seemingly endless stream of public buses and trolley buses on the busy streets. You can ride on one by waiting just a few minutes at any time between 5 a.m. and 11 p.m.

If you want a taxi, you can hail one on the street, or call one through travel agents or from taxi stands stationed in all big hotels and stores, Taxi services are available 24 hours a day.

Generally speaking, your host or travel agent will arrange your transfers from planes or trains to your destinations when you arrive in China.

Public bus fares are based on kilometer rates, while the prices for taxis, mini-buses and coaches are based on kilometers (0.50-0.90 yuan per kilometer) plus any waiting time, varying slightly according to the vehicle and from place to place. The driver will give you tickets with Western numerals indicating the fare to be paid.

When hiring a taxi for sightseeing, try to plan the time you want to spend at any one spot, and ask the driver to wait.

USEFUL POINTS ABOUT ROAD TRAFFIC RULES

Rent-a-car service is just starting in China. You may have a chance to drive a car or ride a motorcycle. The first thing to remember is that you must acquire a driving licence issued by China's Traffic Management section at the Public Security Bureau. Your international or domestic licence is not valid in China. You must seek the approval of the Traffic Management officials. Take along a 35x25mm photograph of head and shoulders and RMB 0.50 (about 0.18 U. S. dollars), together with passport and any other relevant documents.

The Traffic Management section of Beijing Public Security Bureau is at 5, Peixin St., Congwenmenwai. Telephone 743980. Your host organization or travel agent can advise you of offices in other cities.

Remember that the Chinese drive on the right side of the road in designated traffic lanes. Speed limit is 50mph. on motorways and 40mph. in urban areas. You are advised to drive slowly as China's streets are usually crowded.

POST AND TELECOMMUNICATIONS SERVICES

POST

China delivers mail to all countries and regions in the world except south Korea, South Africa and Israel.

Services include letters, postcards, printed matter, registered mail and parcels. All big hotels in major cities have a post office or center providing standard services.

A standard air-mail letter from China to any other country costs 0.80 yuan in postage. Post card is generally 0.70 yuan. An air-mail letter destined for Hongkong or Macao requires 0.10 yuan in stamps.

Insured parcels can be sent to 19 countries, including Yugoslavia, Austria, Italy, France, Britain, the United States and Australia.

Post offices in 22 big cities operate the international Express Mail Service (EMS), which handles nearly all kinds of postal services in a faster way.

The telephone numbers of EMS service points in four major cities are: Beijing 336221, Tianjin 41664, Shanghai 245025, Guangzhou 61325.

Destination countries and regions for international EMS: Argentina, Australia, Brazil, Canada, France, Federal Republic of Germany, Japan, Malaysia, the Netherlands, Singapore, Switzerland, United Kingdom and the United States, as well as Hongkong and Macao.

A domestic letter destined for anywhere inside China requires 0.08 yuan postage, an air-mail one 0.10 yuan and a registered letter 0.20 yuan.

TELECOMMUNICATIONS

TELEPHONE: Rooms at all hotels and leading guest houses are equiped with telephone. Local calls are free when calling from your room's telephone, but when using a phone booth or a public telephone, you have to insert 0.04 yuan or pay the same amount to the phone supervisor.

Domestic and international long-distance calls are priced according to destination and time, the minimum charge being based on a three-minute call. You can make a call by using the hotel telephone, registering through the operator, or by filling out a "long-distance call register slip" at the hotel service desk. Be prepared to pay for it almost immediately and exercise patience when you wait in your room for the connection, which may take some time.

Long-distance phone calls to the United States and Canada cost RMB 7.2 and 9.03 per minute respectively, with a minimum charge for three minutes.

TELEX: Telex services are available in all major Chinese cities covering most destinations. Apart from the main post and telegraph office in the city you are visiting, many hotels also provide the service. Rates to all overseas destinations are RMB 9.60 per minute, with a minimum charge for three minutes.

CABLES: A telegram service is available from all Chinese cities to most overseas destinations. Regular and express rates apply. Cables are charged by the word. Per word to the United States, for example, is RMB 1.30 at regular rate and double for express delivery.

ACCOMMODATIONS

HOTELS

RESERVATIONS

Accommodation can be reserved at a number of hotels such as the Great Wall and Jianguo hotels in Beijing, the Jinling Hotel in Nanjing and the White Swan Hotel in Guangzhou. You may book directly through international long-distance telephone, telegram, or telex or through your travel agent. Your hosts may also be able to book a room for you if you notify them of your date of arrival and length of stay.

ROOM RATES

These vary greatly depending on facilities, services and locations of the hotels. The daily rates for a standard double room in the best hotels in major Chinese cities range from 70 yuan (about 25 U. S. dollars) to 240 yuan (about 90 U. S. dollars). All the best hotels in these cities have air conditioning, private baths, color and closed circuit TV and piped music. But only a few hotels have indoor swimming pools, saunas and gyms.

REGISTRATION

Travelling alone, you should go through at the reception desk the way you would do in the West. If you are a member of a tourist group, you will not have to worry about this, as the tour leader or guide-interpreter of the host organization will complete the registration formalities for you.

ROOM SERVICE

While the Great Wall, the Jinling and the White Swan boast 24-hour room service, other tourist hotels provide a varying degree of room service. For example, the assistants will sell you drinks, collect and deliver laundry and help with mail, messages and telephone calls. In some hotels, breakfast may be served in your room, and even massage services can be administered in your room.

DINING IN THE HOTEL

For inclusive tour groups, all three main meals are served at the hotel restaurants, except for, perhaps, a gourmet meal at a specially-appointed restaurant outside the hotel, at extra charge. But individual visitors or self-paying business groups staying in a Chinese hotel are free to eat either at the hotel restaurant or elsewhere. Restaurants at all the major hotels serve both Chinese and Western food. Some even have French and/or Japanese restaurants. As for Chinese food, each hotel restaurant features one or two distinct schools of Chinese culinary art.

SOME EXTRA ADVICE

Although some Chinese cities claim their tap water is sterilized, to be safe, it is better not to drink from the tap. Hot, boiled water is provided in thermos flasks in the guest rooms. If you want boiled, cold water, call the floor assistant.

If you invite a guest to stay in your room overnight, you should arrange it at the reception desk in advance. Prostitution is strictly banned in China.

Taking souvenirs from a Chinese restaurant or hotel is generally frowned upon. But nowadays, some Chinese hoteliers have begun providing some small souvenirs in the guest rooms, such as matches and envelopes with the hotel name printed on.

Tipping is discouraged at Chinese hotels and restaurants.

CHINESE CUISINE AND EATING OUT

It is hard to say which is the most famous Chinese dishes. One thing is certain though—the foreign visitor's trip to China is always enhanced by the memory he takes home with him of his favorite Chinese dishes.

Indeed, nowhere in the world can one try so many culinary specialities in one country as in China, where cooking is viewed as an art, with great care paid to color, fragrance, taste and presentation of dishes.

There are four major Chinese cuisines: Shandong style or northern cuisine, popular along the Yellow River; Sichuan style or western cuisine, from the upper reaches of the Yangtze River; Jiangsu-Zhejiang style or eastern cuisine, along the Yangtze's middle and lower reaches and the southeastern seaboard; and Guangdong (Cantonese) style or southern cuisine.

However, there is a tremendous number of local variations—probably 50,000 types of dishes in all—and few if any people could claim to have tasted them all.

But it is possible to try dozens of popular specialities during a short stay in China. That does not mean you have to fly 1,000 miles from north to south if you are in Beijing and fancy trying some Guangdong food. Deluxe hotels and restaurants in big cities serve a mixture of all the regional cuisines.

Still, some people argue that authentic local dishes are to be found only in their native homes. That is why in

183

Beijing, Peking Duck is a must. Other popular northern specialities include rinsed mutton in Mongolian hotpot, sweet and sour Yellow River carp (tang cu huanghe li yu), Dezhou braised chicken (Dezhou pa ji), sauteed conches (you bao hai luo), deep-fried prawns (zha da xia) and the Imperial Palace Cuisine.

Equally well known are the Chinese soups. One famous variety, Bird's-Nest soup (qing tang yan cai), is sometimes served as the first major course at a banquet, although soup usually comes at the end of a Chinese meal.

Sichuan province is known as a "land of abundance". So chefs there have made every use of the rich produce and dozens of spices, pepper, ginger and nutmeg that are available.

There are 40 ways to cook the many Sichuan dishes—all of which are characteristically sweet, sour, peppery, spicy, bitter, fragrant or salty, and sometimes all at once.

Among them are strange-flavored chicken shreds (guai wei ji si); Porkmarked Woman's beancurd (ma po dou fu), a very popular dish, cheap as well as delicious, pork shreds with fish seasoning (yu xiang rou si); chicken cubes with chili pepper and soy paste (gong bao ji ding); and spicy braised crucian carp (gan shao ji yu).

The main techniques of eastern cuisine are boiling, stewing and ragout methods. Dishes taste sweet and/or savory. One classic dish is the steamed hilsa herring (qing zheng shi yu), and other popular fish courses include West Lake vinegar fish, fried crispy eel and mackerel soup.

Guangdong cuisine emphasizes freshness, smoothness, tenderness and piquant flavors. It seems that the chefs cook nearly everything that walks, flies or swims.

"Fighting Dragons and Tigers" is probably the most popular of Guangdong game dishes. It is made from cat meat and several kinds of snake. Other favorites include roast suckling pig (pian pi rou zhu), braised beef in oyster sauce (hao you niu rou), crisp skin chicken (cui pi ji) and roast sliced goose (shuang pin pian pi er).

Many foreign visitors say they have tried Chinese food before coming to China. Actually, what they are likely to have had at home is a variety of Guangdong food geared to the Western palate.

Chinese food is usually chopped into small pieces, which can easily be picked up with chopsticks. Chopsticks can present the visitor with the ultimate trial at the dining table. However, they are easy to master after a bit of practice. If you feel uncomfortable with them, knives and forks or spoons are perfectly acceptable substitutes.

Mealtimes: At a formal meal or banquet you will be expected to at least sample every dish. But if you do not like a dish and it is served onto your plate, accept the food graciously and simply leave it untouched. Your plate will soon be whisked away and a clean one provided for the next course.

Beware the Chinese toast "gan bei" ("bottoms up") if you don't want to end up under the table—especially if you are drinking the fiery national tipple "mao tai", which is served at nearly every banquet. Be prepared to offer a toast to your host.

When fruit is served, you know the banquet is over. It is polite to depart about 10 minutes after the towels have been passed and the last cups of tea been drunk.

In restaurants, or anywhere else for that matter, tipping is discouraged.

MEDICAL SERVICES

Should you need medical care, the first thing you should do is to contact your hotel or the Chinese sponsor of your trip. All major hotels in China have clinics or resident doctors to take care of minor ailments and administer first aid.

There are also several fully-equipped modern hospitals especially designed for foreign visitors and overseas Chinese. Experienced doctors trained in Western medicine are assigned to work there. Some are fluent in English, but most are not, so it is advisable to bring an interpreter with you.

Medical care is fairly cheap in China.

If you prefer traditional Chinese medicine, doctors may recommend acupuncture and moxibustion, or some natural herbs, like Ganmao Tea to treat the common cold. These are often extremely effective.

USEFUL ADDRESSES AND TELEPHONE NUMBERS

Head Office and Branches of China International Travel Service (LUXINGSHE):

Head Office:
6, East Chang'an Avenue, Beijing
Tel. 55 7558
Telex: 22350 CITSH CN
Cable: LUXINGSHE BEIJING

Beijing branch:
Chongwenmen Hotel, Beijing
Tel.755017
Telex: 22489 BTTC CN
Cable: 5861 BEIJING

Guangzhou branch:
179 Huanshi Road, Guangzhou
Tel. 69900-2366
Telex: 44150 CITS CN
Cable: 1954 GUANGZHOU

Guilin branch:
14 Ronghu Bei Road, Guilin
Tel. 2648
Telex: 48401 GLITS CN
Cable: 2464 GUILIN

Hangzhou branch:
10 Baoshu Road Hangzhou
Tel. 26971-3072
Telex: 35031 HZT CN
Cable: 1954 HANGZHOU

Kunming branch:
Old building, kunming Hotel, Kunming
Tel. 4992
Telex: 64027 KMITS CN
Cable: 3266 KUNMING

Nanjing branch:
313 Zhongshan Bei Road, Nanjing
Tel. 85921, 86045
Telex: 34119 ITSNJ CN
Cable: 1954 NANJING

Shanghai branch:
33 Zhongshan Dong
Roud, Shanghai
Tel. 210460
Telex: 33277 SCITS
CN
Cable: LUXINGSHE
SHANGHAI

Tianjin branch:
55 Chongqing Dao,
Thanjin
Tel. 34355
Telex: 23242 TJMPG
CN
Cable: 1954 TIANJIN

Xi'an branch:
Yongning Hotel,
Xi'an
Tel. 51221
Telex: 70115 CITSX
CN
Cable: 1954 XI'AN

**China Tourist Offices abroad
and in Hongkong**

China Tourist Office, Tokyo:
Ak-Bldg. 1F. 6-1
Goban-Cho
Chitoda-Ku, Tokyo, -
102,
Japan
Tel. (03) 234-5366

**China Tourist Office,
New York:** Lincoln
Building, 60E42ND
Street, Suite 465
New York, N. Y.
10165
Tel. (212) 867-0271,
(202) 564-8615
Telex: 662142
CITSNYC
Cable: LUXINGSHE,
NEW YORK

China Tourist Office, London:
4, Glentworth Street,
London NWI
Tel. 01-935 9427
Telex: 291221
CTCLONG

**Office du Tourisme de Chine,
Paris:**
7 Rue Sainte Anne,
Paris
Tel. 662142
CITSNYC
Telex: 612866 F
OTCHINE

China Tourist Office, Frankfurt:
Eschenheimer Anlage
28,
D-6000 Frankfurt am
Main-1
Tel. 0611-555292

Luxingshe (International) Hongkong Ltd.:
> 6th Floor, 1. Tower 11. South Seas Centre, 75 Mody Road, Tsim Sha Tsui East, Kowloon, Hongkong
> Tel. 3-7215317 (Six lines)
> Telex: 38449 CITC HX
> Cable: 2320 HONGKONG

China Youth Travel Service (CYTS), the travel department of the All-China Youth Federation

Head Office:
> 23 Dongjiaominx-iang, Beijing
> Tel. 551531
> Telex: 20024 CYTS CN
> Cable: CHINAYTS

Representative Office in Hongkong:
> 904, Nayang Commercial Bank Building, 151 DES VOEUX Road, Central, Hongkong
> Tel. 5410975
> Telex: 61679 YOUTH NX
> Cable: HONSHANC

MAJOR HOTELS

Beijing

Beijing Hotel
> Bast Chang'an Ave.
> Tel. 507766

Jianguo Hotel
> Jainguomen Street
> Tel. 502233

The Great Wall Hotel
> North Donghuan Road
> Tel. 505566

Shanghai

Shanghai Mansion
> 20 North Suzhou Road
> Tel. 246260

Jinjiang Hotel
59 South Maoming Road
Tel. 534242

Heping Hotel
20 East Nanjing Road
Tel. 211244

Guangzhou
Dongfang Hotel
N. Renmin Road
Tel. 69900

Baiyun Hotel
Huanshi Road
Tel. 67700

White Swan Hotel
Shamian Island
Tel. 86968

Hospitals in Major Cities

Beijing
Capital Hospital:
Dongshuaifu Lane, Dongdan Street;
Tel. 553731

Shanghai
Shanghai Huadong Hospital:
257 Yan'an Xilu;
Tel. 563180

Shanghai No. 3 People's Hospital:
145 Shandong Zhonglu;
Tel. 289930

Tianjin
Tianjin Hospital:
Jiefang S. Road;
Tel. 82917

FOREION EMBASSIES AND CONSULATES

Country	Address	Telephone
Embassy of the United States	2 Xiushui Eastern Street, Jianguomen-wai, Beijing	523831
U. S. Consulate-General in Shanghai	1469 Huaihai Zhong Lu., Shanghai	379880
U. S. Consulate-General in Guangzhou	llth Floor, New Building, Dongfang Hotel, Renmin Beilu, Guangzhou	69900
Embassy of Canada	10 Sanlitun Road, Beijing	521475

TEN RECOMMENDED TOURS

Here are 10 regional tours that conveniently link several historical and scenic spots. They can be arranged through CITS:

1. Tour of ancient capitals (Beijing-Xi'an-Zhengzhou-Luoyang-Kaifeng-Zhengzhou-Shanghai). Time: About 17 days.

2. Tour of Confucius's home and Shanghai (Beijing-Tian-in-Qingdao-Jinan-Taishan-Qufu-Shanghai). About 17 days.

3. Tour Tibet (Guangzhou-Chengdu-Lhasa-Guangzhou). About 10 days.

4. Tour of Guilin and the Lijiang River (Guangzhou-Nanning-Liuzhou-Guilin-Guangzhou). About 10 days.

5. Tour along ancient "Silk Road" (Beijing-Lanzhou-Jiuquan-Dunhuang-Urumqi-Xi'an-Guangzhou). About 20 days.

6. Tour of southern scenic cities (Hangzhou-Shanghai-Suzhou-Wuxi-Yangzhou-Nanjing-Beijing-Guangzhou). About 20 days.

7. Tour of central China (Beijing-Chengde-Beijing-Shijiazhuang-Wuhan-Changsha-Guangzhou). About 17 days.

8. Tour of Yungang Grottoes and Inner Mongolia (Beijing-Shijiazhuang-Datong-Wutaishan-Hohhot-Baotou-Beijing). About 21 days.

9. Tour of three Yangtze Gorges (Guangzhou-Chongqing Wuhan-Shanghai). About 14 days.

10. Tour of northeast China (Beijing-Harbin-Jilin-Changchun-Dalian-Shengyang-Guangzhou). About 23 days.

TEMPERATURES IN MAJOR CITIES

Approximate Monthly Temperatures

		Beijing F	Beijing C	Guangzhou F	Guangzhou C	Harbin F	Harbin C	Shanghai F	Shanghai C	Wuhan F	Wuhan C	Xi'an F	Xi'an C
Mean		24	-4	57	14	3	-20	38	3	37	3	30	3
Jan.	High	51	11	82	28	40	4	68	20	70	21	61	16
	Low	-9	-23	32	0	-37	-39	15	-10	1	-17	-5	-21
	Mean	28	-2	58	15	4	-16	40	4	41	5	36	2
Feb.	High	65	18	83	29	52	11	74	24	77	25	70	21
	Low	-17	-27	32	0	-27	-33	18	-8	5	-15	-2	-19
	Mean	40	4	64	18	23	-5	47	8	50	10	46	8
Mar.	High	74	24	88	31	63	17	82	28	85	30	82	28
	Low	10	-12	38	3	-20	-29	22	-6	23	-5	18	-8
	Mean	56	13	71	22	43	6	57	14	61	16	57	14
Apr.	High	86	30	91	33	82	28	92	34	92	34	92	34
	Low	27	-3	46	8	9	-13	32	0	31	-1	25	-4

		Beijing		Guangzhou		Harbin		Shanghai		Wuhan		Xi'an	
		F	C	F	C	F	C	F	C	F	C	F	C
Oct.	Mean	55	13	75	24	43	6	64	18	64	18	56	13
	High	85	32	92	34	80	27	88	31	94	35	91	33
	Low	26	-3	52	11	10	-12	35	2	35	2	31	-1
Nov.	Mean	39	4	67	20	22	-6	55	13	51	11	44	7
	High	76	25	90	32	59	15	83	29	83	29	71	22
	Low	10	-12	42	6	-15	-26	25	4	23	-5	2	-17
Dec.	Mean	27	-3	59	15	4	-16	43	6	43	6	33	1
	High	55	13	85	30	43	6	74	24	74	24	64	18
	Low	-1	-18	35	2	-32	-36	17	-5	16	-9	-3	-20

F=Fahrenheit; C=Centigrade

		Beijing		Guangzhou		Harbin		Shanghai		Wuhan		Xi'an	
		F	C	F	C	F	C	F	C	F	C	F	C
May	Mean	68	20	78	26	58	15	66	19	70	21	67	20
	High	99	38	97	36	96	36	92	34	97	36	100	38
	Low	37	3	58	15	26	-3	44	7	45	7	38	3
June	Mean	76	25	81	27	68	20	74	24	78	26	78	26
	High	103	40	98	37	97	36	98	37	100	38	107	42
	Low	50	10	66	14	41	5	54	12	58	15	49	10
July	Mean	79	26	83	29	73	23	82	28	84	29	80	27
	High	101	39	100	38	98	37	101	39	101	39	106	41
	Low	60	16	71	22	52	11	66	19	63	17	59	15
Aug.	Mean	76	25	83	29	71	22	82	28	83	29	75	26
	High	97	36	102	39	96	36	102	39	103	40	103	40
	Low	54	12	72	22	47	8	67	20	64	18	54	12
Sep.	Mean	67	20	81	27	58	15	75	24	74	24	67	20
	High	89	32	100	38	87	31	99	38	98	40	94	35
	Low	39	4	60	16	30	-1	54	12	50	10	41	5

INDEX

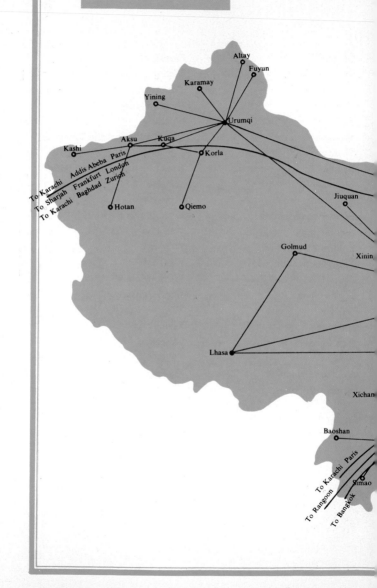

China's air routes

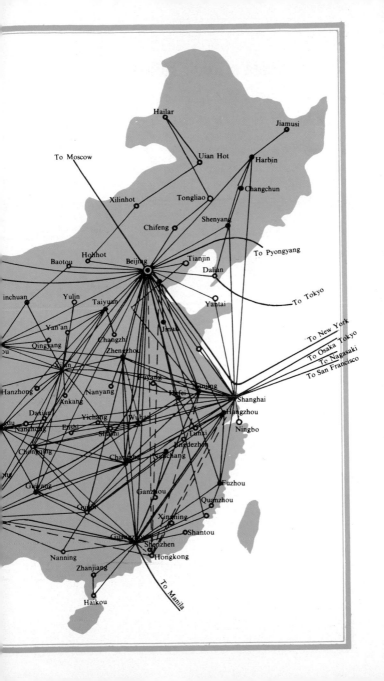

China's trunk railways

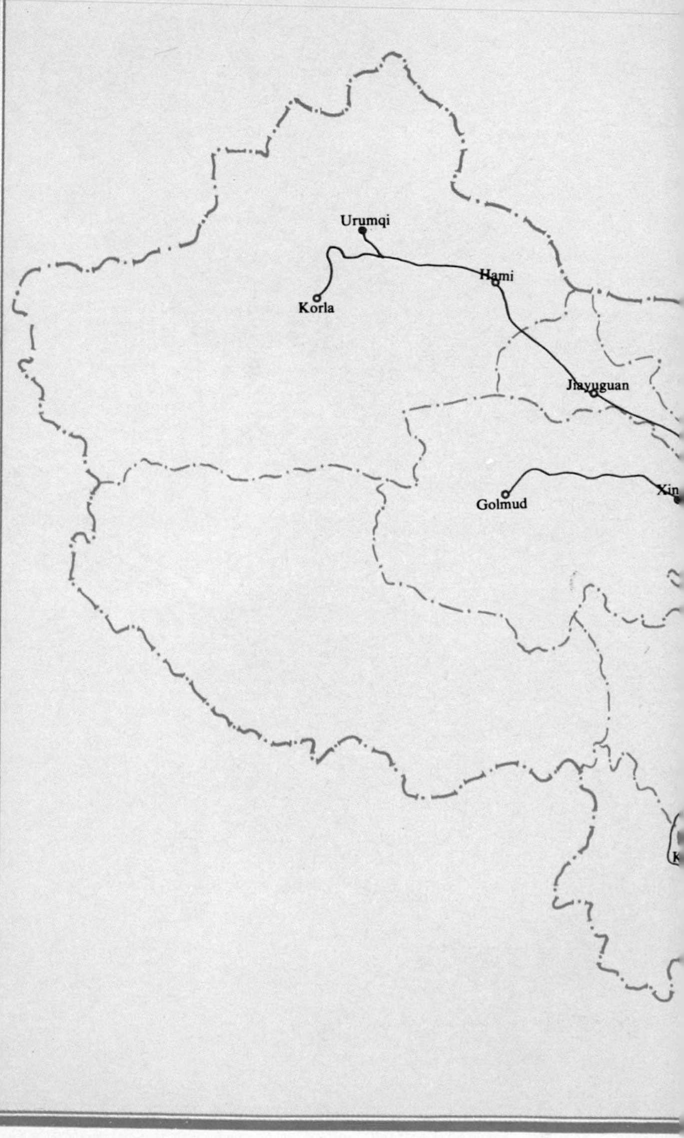

Urumqi

Hami

Korla

Jiayuguan

Golmud

Xin

K

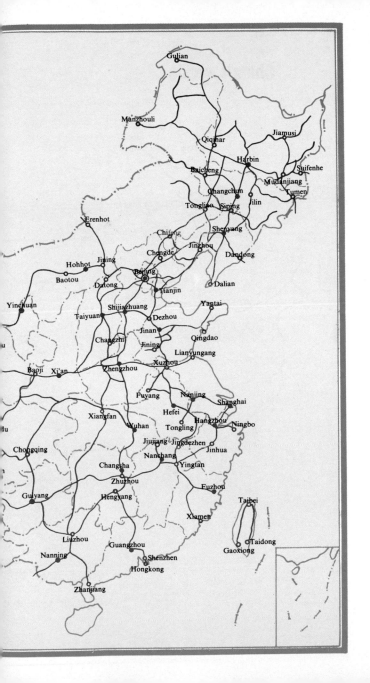

China's roads

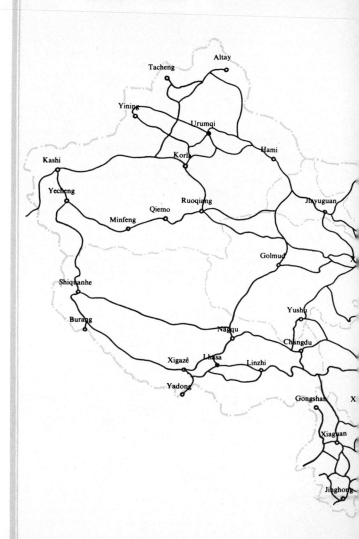

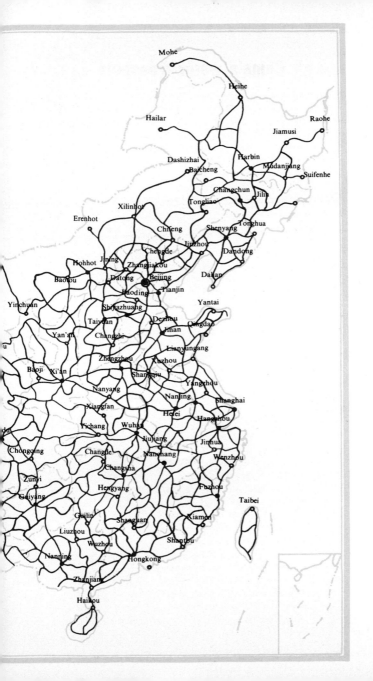

China's water transport

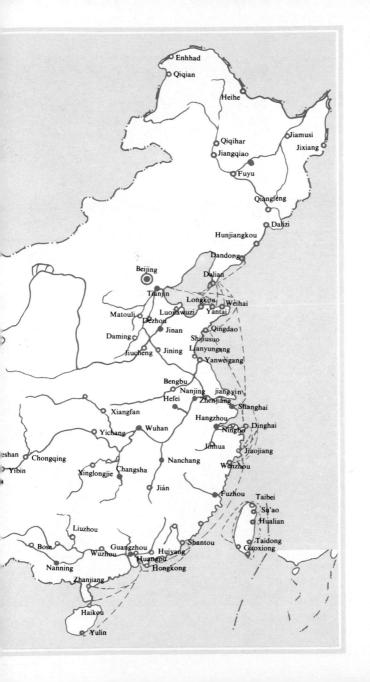

Giant Pandas